D0378247

North American
FLY-FISHING

Fly-Fishing Tactics for 29 of North America's Favorite Freshwater, Anadromous, and Saltwater Game Fish

Bob Newman ■ Illustrated by Susan Newman

Menasha Ridge Press   *Birmingham, Alabama*

Copyright © 1998 by Bob Newman
All rights reserved
Printed in the United States of America
Published by Menasha Ridge Press
First edition
10 9 8 7 6 5 4 3 2 1

Library of Congress Cataloging-in-Publication Data

Newman, Bob, 1958–
    North American fly fishing: fly fishing tactics for 29 of North America's favorite freshwater,
    anadromous, and saltwater game fish / Bob Newman; illustrated by Susan Newman -- 1st ed.
        p. cm.
    ISBN 0-89732-240-1
    1. Fly fishing—North America. I Title
    SH462.N48 1998
    799.1'24'097—dc21   98-10432

Cover design by Grant Tatum
Cover courtesy of Hewes Manufacturing
Interior design by Kandace Hawkinson

Menasha Ridge Press
700 South 28th Street, Suite 206
Birmingham, AL 35233
800-247-9437
www.menasharidge.com

For Mom

Contents

Contents

Part Five: Appendixes

Fly-fishing tackle, gear, accessories, information, and instructional sources

Acknowledgments

THIS BOOK WAS LONG IN THE WRITING, AS MIKE JONES CAN CERTAINLY ATTEST, AND I feel I must thank him first for his patience and understanding. I trust it was worth the wait.

When I first conceived of this book I realized that many people would be involved, and I thank them all here: Scott Anderson, Chuck Ash, Capt. Harold Carlin, Ted Dzialo (Director of the National Fresh Water Fishing Hall of Fame), Capt. Bob Dove, Tom Earnhardt, Brian and Sharon Elder, Andre Godin, Mickey and Maggie Greenwood, Capt. Les Hill, Capt. Brian Horsley, Capt. Mark Houghtaling, Dr. Jay, Capt. Doug Jowett, Capt. Pat Keliher, Capt. Lee Manning, Jennifer and Lars Olsson, Bob Pigott, and Joe Stefanski. This book wouldn't have been possible without your kind interest and assistance.

Special thanks go to my friends George Poveromo and Mark Sosin of *Salt Water Sportsman* for their down-to-earth attitudes and personalities. One might expect nationally recognized anglers like George and Mark to be haughty and arrogant, but nothing could be farther from the truth with these two professionals. I am honored to know and work with them.

Also on the special thanks list are Steve Tooker and Al Maas, and Capt. Bill Harris for their friendship and wisdom.

I am especially indebted to Capt. Bramblett Bradham, Capt. Rodney Smith, and Capt. Richard Stuhr for their phenomenal knowledge, enthusiasm, and kinship.

David E. Petzal, Duncan Barnes, Lionel Atwill, Peter Van Gytenbeek, Frank Golad, Rip Cunningham, Bill Battles, John and Sue Kingsley-Heath, Mark D. Williams, Doc Thompson, Joel Arrington, and Clif and Kim Hannah also have my gratitude.

There is quite a bit of tackle information in here, and this wouldn't have been possible without people like Tom Rosenbauer of The Orvis Company, Randy Swisher and Bill Dawson of Sage, John Duncan of Scott Fly Rods, and John Mazurkiewicz of Catalyst Marketing Services (Scientific Angler).

Acknowledgments

Thanks to Bud Zehmer for the encouragement and friendship.

Of course, my boss, Peder Lund, made sure I had enough time off to cast flies at rude fish, for which I owe him my thanks. Time spent on the water and afield with Peder is the best.

And, as always, thanks to Susie for grinning and bearing it, and to Britta for tagging along.

Introduction

RECENTLY I FOUND MYSELF HIGH IN THE COLORADO ROCKIES CASTING FLIES FOR rainbows, browns, and brookies on the Colorado River and Beaver Creek near Hot Sulphur Springs, and on the Blue River above Dillon Reservoir. Only a few other fly-fishers were on the water and, despite the occasional rising fish, none of us were doing much of anything.

I can't say that about my partner, Mike, who was catching some fine browns on light spinning tackle with spinners. Very annoying, that. I mean, there I was decked out in what surely amounted to more than a thousand bucks worth of tackle and other junk (including all my precious flies), and the guy beside me is tossing a $2 spinner with an ancient Mitchell 300 and a battered fiberglass spinning rod, and he's catching all the trout.

I hate it when that happens.

But that is fly-fishing, and that is just one of the reasons I wrote this book—the mystery of the whole thing. That day on the Colorado and Blue there was only the intermittent midge hatch—tiny black things one would need an electron microscope to tie a reasonable facsimile of. I tied on the closest imitation I had, but nothing doing. I threw Gold-ribbed Hare's Ears, Prince nymphs, a dry Adams, an Elk Hair Caddis, even a Gray Ghost, but the trout were impressed with nothing except Mike's Mepps spinner. Finally, I just drank a beer on the tailgate of my truck and watched Mike catch fat, obviously pagan trout.

It was a long walk back to Broomfield for Mike.

So the mystery of fly-fishing remains intact, as I suspect it will forever. Nevertheless, it is days like last Friday that add to the fascination fly-fishing holds for so many anglers in America. But there is more to the mystery than mere confusion.

Fly-fishing in North America is, more than anything, diverse. One can cast flies for steelhead on the Olympic Peninsula's Sol Duc; largemouth bass at Loxahatchee in the Everglades; spotted seatrout on Texas's Gulf Coast; northern pike on Minnesota's Birch Lake; red drum on Florida's Banana River Lagoon; striped bass on the Kennebec River in Maine; brown trout on

Colorado's North St. Vrain; sockeye salmon along the Alaskan coast; tarpon in the Florida Keys; brookies in unnamed beaver ponds along the Quebec-Maine border; and seemingly countless other game fish hither and yon across this huge land, and only be getting started. This is why, rather than attempting to convince you that, finally, you discovered the fly-fisher to beat all fly-fishers, I sought out some of the most knowledgeable experts in the field to contribute their take on fly-fishing in their areas. Frankly, for one man to insinuate that he is an expert at catching the dozens of species of fish expounded upon in this book—fish found in 50 states under a staggering array of conditions—would be ludicrous and most disingenuous.

This book will teach you many things, but it won't teach you how to fly cast. You see, I don't think it is possible to learn to fly cast from a book (unless your name is Richard Jee, a man who can do many things others can not); you should learn from a friend who is a good teacher or attend a casting school. But this book will give you practical, proven information on myriad species available to the North American fly-fisher, as well as advice on fly-fishing tackle, guides, conservation, and some entertainment in the form of sporadic, babbling, stream-of-consciousness verbal puree.

If you do find I left a chapter out on a certain species (yellowfin tuna and wahoo, for instance), it is only because I feel there just isn't enough interest at this time to warrant a chapter, or that so few people actually intentionally fly-fish for that species. Of course, yellowfin and wahoo are caught on the fly and they are great fighters (and more people should try them), but that doesn't change things at present. Nevertheless, I suspect a revised edition of this book will be in the offing once the first print run is expended; I will add some chapters at that time.

Finally, a word on tackle. You will find in this book that I make certain brand- and model-specific recommendations for rods, reels, lines, and so on. I do so because I have found that gear worthy. I am not sponsored by any fly tackle company whatsoever, so you may be assured that the recommendations I make herein come from experience and not some contractual obligation.

Well, let's get started.

EQUIPMENT AND TECHNIQUE BASICS

Of Rods and Reels

NO DISCUSSION OF FLY RODS AND REELS CAN BE MADE WITHOUT FIRST EXPLORING their reason for being: the fly line. The fly line is absolutely the most important tool the fly-fisher uses, for from it all else comes. Given that, let's take a look at fly lines: how they differ, how they are made, their history, which ones are used for which situations, and so on.

In centuries past, fly lines were constructed of braided horsehair. Fly-fishing historians tell us that early in the 19th century, someone came up with the idea to add silk to the horsehair, and later, about 1870, fly lines began to be constructed of silk without the horsehair.

Things didn't change all that much until 1949, when some crafty anglers at Scientific Anglers found that polyvinyl chloride (PVC) could be applied with heat to a nylon line. This was a huge step forward in the evolution of fly lines. Later, cotton Dacron cores would replace nylon, and additional coatings and cores would appear, such as urethane and Kevlar, the latter of which "body armor" and military combat helmets are made.

In 1961 the American Fishing Tackle Manufacturers Association (AFTMA) and the American Casting Association (ACA) got together to get a handle on all the changes that had occurred in fly lines. Looking for a way to demystify these lines, they came up with a simple code system using numbers and letters to tell the buyer what they were looking at. This code first reflects the line's taper, then the weight, and finally the buoyancy rating. The code is placed on the outside of the line's package.

FLY LINES

The assorted tapers found today include level (L), weight-forward (WF), and double-taper (DT). There are some specialty lines like the shooting head (SH) line (a short, composite line with a heavy casting section that is attached either to a very thin running line made of monofilament or perhaps to a level fly line), and the triangle taper (TT) line (invented by the late Lee Wulff, it steadily increases in diameter from

Fly rods, reels, and lines all have evolved over the years to bring fly-fishers equipment that is truly advanced.

the tip to the 40-foot mark, where it suddenly tapers back down within eight feet and then runs into the running line). Also, as fly-fishers have become more and more specialized and demanding, tapers designed for fishing certain species have popped up, such as Scientific Anglers' tarpon and bonefish tapers.

The level line is all but useless and should be avoided. They sell because they are inexpensive and people buy them without knowing any better.

Weight-forward lines are excellent in that they tend to cast easier because of extra weight in the forward part of the line linked to a running end that is thin. Most fly-fishing situations can be handled with a weight-forward line.

The double-taper line is an excellent line for fishing across stream currents where *mending* (moving the line upstream in a flipping motion without disturbing the fly in order to get a drag-free drift) is required. Mending is facilitated by a double-taper line's thin ends and thicker middle (belly). And because the ends are equidistantly thin, you can reverse the line on the reel when one end becomes worn.

The line's weight, the next part of the code, is taken from the number of grains in the first 30 feet of line. This ranges from 1 to 15. A 1-weight line would be used for the most delicate and fine trout fishing on tiny streams for dainty trout, while a 15-weight would be used on marlin, big tuna, and other such game fish.

Finally comes the buoyancy of the line. A floating line (F) floats on the surface because of air cells injected into the PVC coating. An intermediate line (I) is meant to have neutral buoyancy; it sinks a little ways and stops.

The sinking lines (S) have powdered lead or some other heavy substance added to the coating to make them sink. The sink rates vary, running from one foot every second to about 10 feet every second. Sink-tip lines (F/S) are lines with a floating belly and a tip section (between 10 and 30 feet) that sinks. As far as line lengths go, they all range from about 82 feet to a little more than 100 feet.

All this means that an AFTMA fly line code reading DT-5-F is a double-taper, 5-weight, floating line. A WF-12-F/S is a weight-forward, 12-weight, sink-tip. A L-7-F is a level, 7-weight, floating line. A WF-9-I is a weight-forward, 9-weight, intermediate line. A WF-6-S is a weight-forward, 6-weight, sinking line.

Choosing A Fly Line

In fly-fishing, as in any other type of fishing, you get what you pay for when it comes to fly lines. When you pay $5 or $6 for a fly line, you get about $5 or $6 worth of performance. On the other hand, when you pay substantially more for a line made by reputable, proven manufacturers like Scientific Anglers, Fenwick, Wulff, Orvis, L.L. Bean, and Teeny, you get a line you know you can trust, one that will perform as it was meant to perform. Don't ever skimp on a fly line.

The best line to start with is a weight-forward floating line because it is so versatile. If you will be fishing moving streams and rivers, buy a double-taper floating line. As you learn more about the art of fly-fishing and get into more specific situations, you will need to get other lines. For instance, when fishing fairly well below the surface of still waters, a slow-sinking line is used. If you are in a situation where you have to get the line down faster, like in a moving river, a faster sink rate is required. If you are casting heavy flies into the wind, you may want to opt for a shooting head. When you want the fly to sink but most of the fly line to remain on the surface, like in many salmon and trout fishing situations on rivers and streams, you will want a sink-tip. And when fishing in bright sun and hot temperatures, you could benefit from using a line that is ultraviolet resistant; UV light breaks down the PVC coating on standard fly lines.

When beginning to fly-fish, first consider the species of fish you expect to spend the most time chasing, but remember that tuned angling skills make it possible to catch very big fish on comparatively light fly-fishing tackle. In the Florida Keys, you will be after bonefish, barracuda, tarpon, permit, cobia, and dolphin, among many other species. You will need a 10- to 13-weight for average tarpon and bigger barracuda (an 8- or 9-weight for smaller "ditch" tarpon), but a 6- to 9-weight will suffice for the others, generally speaking. If you intend to pursue bluegill in farm ponds or small trout in tight streams, use a wispy 1- to 4-weight. Bass and bigger trout anglers find cause for fly rods in the 5- to 7-weight. Inshore fly-fishing for spotted seatrout, red drum, striped bass, and bluefish sees a 7- to 9-weight on deck. Northern pike and muskie insist upon an 8- to 10-weight.

Right about now you must realize that if you intend to catch many or perhaps even all of these species of fish, you are going to spend some money gearing up. But that's part of the fun, even if it takes years to get there.

Backing

Backing is the emergency line separating the fly reel's arbor from the fly line itself. Normally made of Dacron, it fills the reel's spool and gives the fly-fisher plenty (well, usually) of extra line to fight a fish on.

Leaders

The leader is what separates the fly line from the fly. It allows the fly to act more naturally, doesn't scare nervous fish as easily as a fly line can, and helps to prevent the fly from striking the water so hard that the fish runs off (although in some fishing situations you *want* the fly to hit hard). Most leaders are made of nylon monofilament; they can come pre-packaged and knotless, or you can construct your own with assorted sections of monofilament of various tensile strengths. They come in many lengths, and today you can find specialty leaders to use for specific situations, like with a wet fly (special wet fly leaders sink along with the fly), toothy fish, or what have you. Most leaders run from 6–15 feet, but in some instances, as when fishing sinking lines in murky or roily water, you may need only a 3-foot leader.

Tippet is a section of special leader added to the end of the leader where you will be tying your fly. It is used to add delicacy or strength to the whole system, depending on what you are fishing for.

Leaders and tippets are rated by an "X" code with a corresponding number. The lower the X number, the thicker the tippet's diameter. The diameter of the leader and/or tippet can be crucial in presentation of the fly. Check the package for the tensile strength.

FLY RODS

The creation of a fly rod is a science unto itself, and one that is constantly evolving and improving. There is no shortage of fly rod manufacturers nowadays, with names like Orvis, Sage, Scott, Thomas & Thomas,

Modern graphite fly rods are very sensitive and strong.

Redington, L.L. Bean, Scientific Anglers, Winston, G. Loomis, and many more being well known and quite respected. This proliferation of fly rod manufacturers forces the other guy to always be thinking and coming up with new ideas, manufacturing techniques, and practical features. Adding to this is the remarkable explosion of interest in fly-fishing since the late 1980s. But before we can look at what rod you should buy for what type of fly-fishing, and just as importantly what rod you *shouldn't* buy, we must look to yesterday.

Fly rods have been constructed of steel, boron, fiberglass, bamboo, and graphite over the years. Steel and boron have fallen by the wayside, and bamboo remains extremely expensive (although Orvis still makes a magnificent bamboo rod for under $1,000), but fiberglass and graphite have survived well, especially graphite, which is sensitive and strong, yet light. Today, graphite is the only way to go when considering a fly rod. It certainly beats the performance of steel, which was popular earlier in this century and was eventually replaced by fiberglass. Boron fly rods briefly came into their own in the early 1980s, but did not pan out in the long run; graphite proved to be far superior across the spectrum of performance. Bamboo rods are for people with far too much money. Fiberglass rods are still readily available in the marketplace today and improvements have made them sensitive and light, but even the most well-crafted fiberglass fly rod can't compare to a reputable manufacturer's bargain basement graphite wand.

Every fly-fisher yearns for the creation of a single fly rod that can handle every fly-fishing situation; it could perform wonderfully for bonefish on the flats, steelhead in the riffles, bass in the lily pads, brown trout in pocket water, snook in the mangroves, bream in the brush piles, dolphin in the sargassum, and tarpon in the channels. Obviously, such a rod is only a wish, and the chance of one ever coming into being is nil. This means the fly-fisher is left to pick and choose very carefully among myriad specialty rods that have a wide range of actions, lengths, and line-handling abilities.

Actions

Do not confuse fly rod actions with those described on spinning rods—they are two different things. The action of a fly rod refers to how it bends along the blank (its foundation), not the classification of line it is designed to handle, as with many spinning and bait casting rods.

TIP-FLEX (FAST ACTION): A tip-flex fly rod has a high degree of stiffness <u>and</u> tip action, meaning it bends in the cast only about one-third of the way down the blank. (There are also very fast action rods that bend only about one-quarter of the way down the rod.) A tip-flex rod is able to cast a fly line farther with less effort than mid-flex and full-flex rods because the rod's *modulus* (degree of stiffness) is greater. However, it is not as accurate as its slower brethren. Tip-flex rods are best employed by more experienced casters, since they aren't very forgiving when it comes to mistakes made during the cast, i.e., reduced efficiency.

MID-FLEX (MEDIUM ACTION): The mid-flex fly rod splits the difference between tip-flex and full-flex rods by loading to about the middle of the blank during casting. This action does forgive more than fast action and is therefore used frequently in fly casting instruction for beginners. It is more accurate than the fast action, too, but does not generate the power of the tip-flex rod.

FULL-FLEX (PROGRESSIVE ACTION): The full-flex rod easily bends just about to the butt when casting. This is the action favored by fly-fishers who target spooky trout in small, tight streams where long casts aren't called for but great accuracy is. Full-flex, also known as parabolic or slow action, is demonstrated by a rod bending progressively more from tip to butt as the load is increased. (When we speak of "loading" the rod we refer to the power of the cast and the weight of the fly line that is in the air beyond the rod's tip-top, plus the weight of the leader, tippet, and fly. So, a full-flex rod will bend more and more as load is increased and power is applied.)

DAMPING: A note here on damping, which is how quickly the fly rod's tip stops vibrating after a quick movement; inertia, bend, rod stiffness, and drag are all part of this equation. Damping has been the bane of rod engineers ever since they realized that the longer it takes for the tip's wiggle to stop, the more wiggles form in the line; this results in lost casting efficiency.

All this has led engineers to search like mad for a way to get the rod tip to stop wiggling more quickly after a cast or mend. It now appears that The Orvis Company won the race by turning out their 1995 Trident Series of fly rods, which substantially increases the rate at which wiggle dies out. No doubt other manufacturers are developing construction techniques of their own to follow suit. Orvis intends to work this new technology into all their rods eventually, and they have already begun refining the Tridents.

Lengths

Rod lengths run from 5 1/2 feet to 16 feet, with 8 1/2 feet or so being most common. The smallest fly rod I have ever come across was a tiny 5 1/2-foot rod owned by my friend John Kingsley-Heath, a retired professional hunter who enjoyed a 30-year career running safaris and doing control work in East Africa. In front of a pleasant fire in a 400-year-old hearth bracketed by two massive tusks of ivory, I slid the dainty travel rod from its cloth and put it together. Sipping a glass of fine, single malt scotch (the British are hoarding all the good stuff, you know), I admired the little rod and assumed it was crafted many years ago to fish narrow streams, most of which are now too filled with pesticides and other run-off poisons from the farms that dot the countryside to hold any trout. Studying the rod in the glow of the fire, I wondered if it would ever feel the weight of a trout again.

Generally speaking and all other things being equal, short rods are less efficient during casting because they are not capable of loading properly in order to throw the line. Seven feet is about as short as I like to go, and I use such short rods only when fishing the smallest of flies in tight quarters, such as fishing a size 20 Pheasant Tail nymph on the West Branch of Maine's Nash Stream (though there are places along this stream where I have desperately wished for a 6-footer). Nor do I like casting a rod longer than 10 feet; I find annoying and frustrating the added weight and wind resistance, regardless of the grade of graphite in the rod's construction. Nevertheless, the bottom line is to use the rod *you* like best for the situation, not what some outdoor writer says you should like.

Weight

When selecting a rod weight, consider the size and strength of the fish you intend to catch, what types and sizes of flies you will use, and the conditions you will fish under (tight mountain streams, broad Western rivers, flats, offshore, farm ponds, big lakes, etc.). For smallish trout on small waters that require delicate presentation, a 1-weight rod will do. Fly-fishing for typical trout or bream, or fishing on mid-sized streams and other waters suggests a 5-weight rod, while a 7-weight is a fine, classic bass rod. A 10-weight rod is great for light tarpon or false albacore, and a 15-weight rod is meant for tuna and billfish. It is fairly easy to pick the right weight; simply remember to choose a rod that can perform properly. Too heavy a rod and the fight will not be enjoyed; too light a rod and the fish will overpower you, resulting in too long a fight and an exhausted fish that may not survive release.

Materials

Graphite.

Remember that word, because the vast majority of fly rods are made from graphite nowadays. Skip the heavier, clumsy, fiberglass rods. Yes, the latter are much less expensive, but they just don't cast nearly as well—and that means frustration and disappointment. Go ahead and buy yourself a bamboo fly rod if you must. Yes, it will run you between $1,000 and $2,000, but they are lovely and traditional.

Graphite is strong, efficient in the physics sense, and very sensitive, and it has all the other attributes needed to make a good fly rod. Naturally, the higher the grade of graphite, the more expensive the rod. You can buy a decent graphite fly rod for as little as $100 or thereabouts, even less if you catch them on sale.

Grips

Too many beginning fly-fishers fail to consider the grip on the rod they are considering.

Grips come in varying diameters and shapes for varying sizes of hands and personal tastes, numerous species and sizes of fish, and different conditions on the water. Large hands often like a full wells grip (which also gives the angler the ability to put additional thumb pressure on the grip); medium-sized hands frequently like either a half wells (*not* a reverse half wells, which is a poor design, ergonomically speaking) or cigar; smaller hands seem to prefer the superfine. Again, the choice is yours.

Cork grips are the industry standard. If you will be handling many slimy fish during a day's fishing wipe your hands on a rag to remove the slime before you grip the rod again. Then again, if you are releasing the fish, you shouldn't be handling it in such a way that the fish's protective slime comes off on your hand.

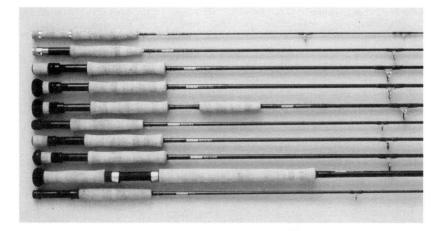

Grips are designed to handle the type of fly-fishing being performed, with an eye to the species, size of fish, conditions at the time, and even the size of the fly-fisher's hand.

Rings And Things

To go into any more detail on the parts of a fly rod here would be pointless. Suffice it to say that any good introductory, broad-brush book on how to get started fly-fishing (and fly casting) will tell you about the intricacies of the fly rod, touching on such things as reel seats designs, guides, hook keepers, and so on. As this is not an introductory fly-fishing book per se, and it certainly isn't broad-brushed, we'll skip such minutiae and move along.

FLY REELS

On May 12, 1874, the founder of The Orvis Company, Charles F. Orvis, was granted a patent on his new Trout Reel. Virtually all fly reels since are based upon the principles that set this reel apart from all others. While materials used to make the first reels (nickel silver and nickel-plated brass) have changed (to aluminum), it is still very evident that Mr. Orvis changed the face of fly-fishing forever.

Today's serious reels are light and durable, and capable of taking tremendous pressure from powerful fish trying to fuse the reel's drag system. Whereas the old adage that describes a fly reel as a place to store fly

World-class reels have superior drags and gear systems that can handle the most demanding fish.

line still rings true for small, less-than-powerful game fish like bluegill and many trout, when you intend to fight fish off the reel, like red drum, steelhead, bonefish, and permit, the reel becomes much more important, and the most important aspect of that reel is the drag system it employs.

Regardless of the type of drag system your reel features (disk or ratchet-and-pawl), make sure it functions smoothly (no skipping) from the moment it engages to the moment you land the fish. (Changes in friction applied during a fight will likely cost you the fish.) It must be heat-resistant throughout the fight. When completely disengaged, the drag should be just that—*completely disengaged*—so that line runs freely off the spool. And the drag adjustment knob must be easily accessed and used, yet out of the way and not cumbersome or awkward. Reels with a palming rim allow the angler to apply additional drag with his palm, a nice touch that can come in handy.

The reel should be matched to the rod for balance. Too heavy or too light a reel for the rod will hinder casting and playing of the fish.

Now that you know the basics—and then some—of your tackle, let's check on guides and other matters.

Of Guides and Gear, And This and That

GUIDES

THIS BOOK CONSISTS OF ADVICE FROM MYSELF, YES, BUT ALSO FROM MANY GUIDES (as well as professional anglers like Mark Sosin and George Poveromo) who make their living fishing.

Fly-fishing guides have grown in number with the increased interest in fly-fishing. Naturally, not all are the kind you would hope for, but there are ways to weed out the bad guys from the good guys; I have found that just a little effort goes a long way toward this end.

Flip open a magazine like *Fly Fish America, Fly Fishing in Salt Waters,* or *Fly Rod & Reel* and you will find a host of fly-fishing guides advertising their services. Unfortunately, you cannot judge a guide by his advertisement. For example, I am familiar with an outdoor writer who used to live in one New England state while writing for another state's outdoor magazine and tried to give the impression he lived in that state. The information he passed on in his column was no more than rehashed information from another writer's column in the same magazine, and everyone knew it. A few years later he suddenly moved to the Florida Keys and soon thereafter he was taking out large ads in the fly-fishing periodicals. These adds gave one the impression he was native to the Keys and had spent decades catching giant fish there, and a hell of a lot of them at that. Now, maybe this guy is the greatest guide south of Port Everglades, but somehow I doubt it.

You can't judge a guide from his ad.

So what to do? Write, fax, e-mail, or call the guide you are considering hiring and ask him for 10 references. Contact all 10 and ask about the guide. Was he on time and at the boat before you were? Did other guides greet him nicely in the morning? Was he dressed in clean, functional clothing? Were his boat and tackle shipshape? Was he enthusiastic and willing to instruct and give advice in such a way that he didn't sound annoyed or like he thought you were an idiot? Did he bring along soft drinks, water, and coffee? Did he tell you beforehand what items (lunch, tackle, clothing, gear, etc.) *you* should bring? Was he quick with the net or gaff? Did he point out fish you missed? Did he ask for his fee up front or wait until you got back? (A guide who demands money up front is to be avoided; he wants it up front because he suspects you aren't going to catch anything.) If you kept some fish, did he clean them for you free of charge? Did he ask about your accommodations and whether or not they were acceptable? Did he recommend any restaurants?

These questions need to be asked and the vast majority should be answered in the affirmative (except for the question about collecting his fee up front).

You also should ask how the fishing was, another reason why 10 clients should be queried, since *every* guide has the occasional off day. This way you play the odds. If half or more say they caught little or nothing, look for another guide.

Keep in mind, too, that these are just some of the questions that could be asked.

Oh, and ask the guide what his fee is for a half, three-quarter, and full day's fishing, and then check with other guides in the area to see if his prices are reasonable.

Finally, ask if the guide was drinking any alcoholic beverages. Now, there are two potentially good answers here, depending on your personal tastes and needs. First, if you don't drink and don't want your guide to have any either, then hopefully the answer will be no. Second, if you do drink and want—nay, *demand*—some beer aboard, hopefully the answer will be yes.

I won't even get *in* a boat with a sober guide.

GEAR

Long ago (about 30 years ago, if you must know), my father handed me my first fly rod on a hill overlooking Maine's St. Croix River. I have no idea who made it or what species of reel was attached, and I suspect the line had been on there for quite some time (and don't even ask me about the backing), but that old rod caught me hundreds of frantic smallmouth bass on Washington County's Crawford Lake and many a fine brook trout, which have been accurately called "living jewels," from the myriad brooks and streams around Red Beach, Robinson, and Calais. It served me well and I never gave any thought to what it was made of (almost certainly fiberglass), how much it had cost, and what company made it.

Today, the first thing I look at when I pick up a fly rod is the manufacturer's name. This is out of habit, for I am at the point now where I have become familiar with every major fly rod manufacturer in America and know by the name whether or not it is a quality rod. So when I look at the name, I know why it might cost a few hundred dollars. It all has to do with reputation, time spent crafting the rod, the quality of the workmanship and materials, the experience and ingenuity of the designers, and more. Happily, insofar as fly rods and reels go, you most often get what you pay for nowadays.

Don't get me wrong. I am not advocating your going out and dropping a few grand on a selection of fly rods. What I am saying is, purchasing a single high-quality rod (and some good instruction) will eventually make you a more efficient fly caster, and therefore, eventually, help you become a better fly-fisher. Avoid going out and spending the same amount of money on a dozen mass-produced discount rods. A good, forgiving rod and a patient, attentive instructor are worth their weight in gold, whereas a garbage rod and the same instructor will produce a handicapped fly caster who will spend more time and energy than necessary on learning the basics and achieving reasonable results.

Reels are a little different because you can buy a perfectly good reel for less than $30 if you will be using it for bream and small trout. On the other hand, a $30 reel will last 30 seconds when thrown into the *mosh pit* with a 20-pound false albacore or a 30-pound jack before it goes to critical mass and melts down in your hands.

As for lines, the worst thing you can do is spend a lot of money on a fine rod and reel and then pay $5 for a cheesy fly line. Cheesy fly lines beget cheesy casts and presentations, and worse. Always stick with a brand name line made by a respected manufacturer. This doesn't mean you should spend $75 on a line you will be using for farm-pond bream. It does mean you need to buy lines that match the strength of the fish and the conditions in which you will be fishing.

And then there is all that other stuff you are going to need, like flies (thousands and thousands of them, as my wife, Susan, is so keen on point-ing out), vests, waders, float tubes, hip boots, thermometers, sunglasses, hats, sunblock, nippers, scales, wading staffs, books, magazine subscriptions, reel and rod cases, fly boxes, forceps, leader straighteners, floatants, hook sharpeners, retractors, strike indicators, boats, leader wallets, and about a thousand other crucial tools of the trade (or, "tools of the fool," according to Susan). Face it: This could get expensive. Live with it.

But you shouldn't run out and start buying indiscriminately if you are just getting started. Decide what species you will be fishing for most often, and buy only what you need to figure them out and fish for them effec-tively. As you spread out and begin fishing more waters for different species under varying conditions, ask around, read a lot, and then get what you need.

SCHOOLS AND INSTRUCTORS

It is important to check out fly-fishing schools and instructors just as you would a guide, but there is one big difference, that being the fact that you can rely upon long-established schools conducted by major outfits. This is akin to buying a Mercedes or BMW: You need not ask if the car is built well. It is. Ask around for comments and results from smaller organizations and private schools.

OK, let's hit the water.

FRESHWATER GAME FISH

Largemouth Bass

3

Steve Tooker
Steve Tooker Guide Service
Walker, Minnesota

Al Maas
Al Maas Guide Service
Walker, Minnesota

THE POPULARITY OF THE LARGEMOUTH BASS IS MADE CLEAR BY THE PROLIFERATION of bass fishing shows on Saturday morning, the number of bass boats being manufactured and sold, the amazing quantities of bass-fishing tackle found everywhere, and the phenomenal success of the Bass Anglers Sportsman Society (BASS). But while fly-fishing for largemouth bass is popular, one simply can't say the sport has anywhere near reached the prevalence of fly-fishing for red drum or, for that matter, baitcasting for bucketmouths.

I'm not sure why this is. Perhaps there are just so many other species available that interest in catching largemouths on the fly has yet to explode. Nevertheless, those familiar with the thrill a big *hawg* can give a fly-fisher know that the largemouth bass is a fighter worthy of much attention and effort.

Largemouths can be caught on the fly in every state in the Lower 48. They frequently feed ravenously, fight well, and can survive in various types of water (from rivers and streams to swamps, lakes, ponds, reservoirs, and even drainage ditches). And, perhaps best of all, anyone can suddenly find themselves tied into a double-digit brawler when they least expect it, like when casting rubber spiders for bluegill.

If you haven't tried fly-fishing for largemouths, you need to.

SEASONS AND SIZES

Largemouth bass are some of the most seasonally affected freshwater game fish, depending upon where they are. For instance, I spent some of my youth catching largemouths in the Everglades and in the canals of south Florida around Sunrise and Plantation, where one can cast a fly to them 365 days a year and fully expect to catch several, with one or two weighing 4 or 5 pounds. The famous Florida strain of largemouths in those parts always seemed to have plenty of feed available—big golden shiners, bream, and crayfish—and there was so much water and so much cover that they couldn't help but thrive.

The rest of my youth I spent in Maine, where fly-fishing for largemouths in central and southern ponds began in late May after the ice went out and lasted into early October. I quickly learned that, unlike in Florida, Maine largemouths weren't in every body of freshwater you threw a fly into. And they seemed more temperamental, too, becoming very active in June and September but seeming to become stubborn in the dead of summer.

Later in life I would find myself fly-fishing for largemouths in many different situations, and I soon picked up on the fact that one must really know the water if one expects to regularly catch big largemouths on the fly. I found that in San Diego's Otay Reservoir giant streamers were more productive than poppers when worked in the timber; that weedless deer-hair bugs were the ticket on Minnesota's Leech Lake and Maine's Pleasant Pond; and that poppers and rubber spiders were excellent on many North Carolina farm ponds.

Whereas it is true that any of these flies will catch bass on any of these waters (and all other largemouth bass waters), knowing which fly is *most likely* to produce a trophy bass on a particular water is crucial. The key to all this, of course, is opening your mouth and asking questions, coupled with paying attention to what other successful fly-fishers are doing and what is going on in and on the water, i.e., are the bass feeding on golden shiners deep in the thickest sawgrass? Are they feeding on rainbow trout a foot long? Or are they gulping leeches along a breakline?

Largemouths weigh up to 21 pounds or so, but any fish that

Large poppers often mean large bass, like this one taken by Steve Tooker.

weighs more than 10 pounds is considered worth bragging about. Some waters—even small farm ponds—hold bass averaging 3 or 4 pounds (such as Florida's St. Johns River), while others only contain fish that average a pound or so, such as North Carolina's New River. The San Diego chain of lakes, on the other hand, is home to giant bass and plenty of them, and experts believe the next International Game Fish Association (IGFA) all-tackle record large-mouth will in fact come out of one of these lakes. One thing is clear, despite all the other factors involved in turning out big bass: If the bass have lots of large prey to feed on, like golden shiners and trout, they will likely grow to world-class proportions.

TACKLE

You must consider the average size of the bass in the water you are on and the conditions you will be fishing under when determining the rod and leader best suited for that water.

Rods generally run from a 5-weight for smallish bass in protected waters to a 9-weight for casting hefty, wind-resistant bugs into a stiff wind and thick aquatic vegetation like masses of lily pads, milfoil, and broad-leaved pondweed. Lengths and actions vary accordingly.

There is no need for a $400 reel. Bass do not make long runs and they seldom burn up a reel. A Scientific Anglers System 2, Lamson DCA-3, L.L. Bean Angler, Orvis Clearwater, or equivalent reel is all that is needed.

Most largemouths are taken on the surface, but you will need more than a single weight-forward or double-taper floating line to consistently catch them. There will be times when a sink-tip is an absolute must, and sometimes a full-sink line is required to get at bass holding 10 feet or so near bottom, where they may be eating leeches and crayfish and have no interest in going to the surface for a bug that has fallen in the water.

Leaders are determined by the average size of the bass and the struc-ture they are in, plus the size of the fly you are casting. Tossing a bulky deer-hair bug at 4-pound bass in a cabbage patch requires a leader no longer than the rod you are using. The butt is most important in such a sit-uation, since a stout (but not stiff) butt is needed to turn the big fly over. You can work out your own formulas, but here's an idea: For an 8 1/2-foot, 8-weight rod that will be casting large bugs, I might go with an 8-foot leader with a 20-pound butt section about 3 1/2 feet in length. My next section will be about a foot and a half of 15-pound test, followed by 2 feet of 12-pound test, and finally a foot of 10-pound-test tippet. Yes, this adds up to a total of 5 knots along the leader (including the nail knot and what-ever knot I used to tie the fly to the tippet), but the system is pretty reliable. Is such a system an absolute must? Certainly not. I have taken hundreds of decent largemouths on knotless right-out-of-the-package leaders. However, when you do break a fish off with this system, you seldom lose the entire leader, and replacing the broken section is quick and easy if you just take the time to pre-make some leaders and keep them with you.

Flies for bass include nearly everything under the sun, so don't restrict yourself to traditional bugs, poppers, and rabbit-fur flies. Tie or buy some saltwater flies like Rattle Rousers, Bonito Bunnies, Clousers, and even tarpon flies and give them a try. Also, I often throw large nymphs like the Kauffman's Stone and assorted hellgrammite imitations and frequently have found them highly productive. Naturally, old standbys like a Dahlberg Diver or Dave Whitlock's creation known as the Mouserat often do the job admirably. (Dave Whitlock is the nation's leading bass expert when it comes to flies and fly-fishing.)

Al Maas is a guide who knows which leaders work under tough conditions.

TACTICS

We can begin by looking at two of the most important factors in fly-fishing for bass (and these two factors, I am pleased to say, were realized by Steve Tooker and Al Maas in Minnesota while I was discovering them in Maine, California, Florida, and North Carolina before we ever met): what depth the fish are in and what the structure is like. From these two factors all else comes. Factors like the pre-spawn, spawn, post-spawn, cloud cover, forage, pH, water temperature, wind, and so on are all secondary if you can first determine how deep the bass are and what structure they are orienting on. Fortunately, largemouths taken on the fly are usually in water less than 10 feet deep (oftentimes much less) and the structure they are holding on is frequently either plainly visible or easily deduced.

Let's begin by looking at the surface, which provides the most exciting action on the fly because largemouths tend to explode on a fly presented there.

The Surface

The two most prevalent types of surface flies are poppers made of cork, balsa, or even plastic, and deer-hair creations. First poppers.

Designed to attract the largemouth's attention with sound created by the popper's concave face, these bugs *blooop* when twitched and yanked properly, diving slightly down as they do so (if designed right). Many have rubber legs jutting out from the side and nearly all have a few feathers sticking out the back. Bass use their sensitive lateral line to detect these sounds, which to them must sound like a frog, large insect, or wounded baitfish struggling on the surface. (I smile at fly-fishers who claim to know precisely what kind of prey the bass thinks is making a noise. In actuality, no one but the bass knows this and it is highly unlikely he is saying to himself, *Yum! Look at that big cicada that has fallen out of that elm tree. Mmmm, mmmm, good.* Realistically speaking, the bass' instincts are what really determine its actions rather than cognizant thought. This instinct works like ours. We know as a matter of instinct and experience that rocks, ink wells, fax machines, and computer chips are not food, and a bass' instinct and experiences tell it what is probably edible and what isn't.) A largemouth that "hears" this noise will most often slowly turn toward the sound and approach it cautiously to see if it looks edible and appetizing, although sometimes they simply attack it instantly in what experts feel is an instinctive reflex action akin to something like, *Food! Eat it now!* But in most cases the bass will drift toward the popper and then bolt forward, open its mouth wide, and inhale, then quickly turn away.

Pencil poppers have thin, elongated bodies with feathers at the end and no rubber legs or other accoutrements to speak of. The face may be concave, or flat with an overbite of sorts.

Although technically not "poppers" because they don't "pop," flat-faced cork and balsa bugs are often lumped in with true poppers perhaps because calling them all one thing is easier. However, these are more accurately termed "splashers" or "pushers," since they splash and push water ahead of them when retrieved. Sometimes the bass will demand one or the other, and you have to know the difference and know how to exploit that difference.

An assortment of Muddler Minnows should always be at hand.

There are other, more unusual designs, but for cork and balsa these descriptions should suffice. A selection of half a dozen of each in various sizes and colors will almost always be sufficient. Now let's look at deer-hair bugs.

Bass flies made of deer hair greatly increased in popularity in the 1980s (even though the first deer-hair bugs made available to the general public were created in the 1920s), and nowadays every serious fly-fisher targeting largemouth bass carries flies like the Dahlberg Diver, Umpqua Swimming Frog, Most Whit Hair Bug, and Muddler Minnow. Deer hair makes for some fine and very versatile flies, and every fly-fisher after bass needs a selection.

Cork and balsa bugs and flies made from deer hair are excellent in many situations where the largemouths are in shallow water holding either in or just above or beside structure. Fortunately, unlike trout that have seen many flies and seem to learn to tell the difference between a caddisfly and an Elk Hair Caddis, bass that have been heavily fished over do not seem to be as intelligent. If you cast something at them that looks and acts like food, they may very well jump on it regardless of how many other flies they have seen lately. I am convinced that, unlike crafty browns and rainbows that often demand an exact replica of the flies hatching at that very moment, hungry largemouth bass will eat most anything that looks and acts real. Part of the reason for this may be the difference between a mayfly, caddisfly, stonefly, or midge hatch, and a frog, bait fish, or insect that wanders into a bass' territory.

Trout holding in moving water focus tightly on hatches and don't often move out of their feeding lane or take something that doesn't fit what is happening on the water at that moment, i.e., trout won't often leave the slip-stream behind the rock during a massive green drake hatch to swallow a midge. But a largemouth will readily move 10 feet to one side to get at a golden shiner. The bass is a predator of opportunity more often than the trout.

Therefore, the key to drawing a surface strike from a largemouth is to successfully imitate something the bass will believe is real and worth the effort (meaning it will get more energy from eating the thing than it spent capturing it).

Key to all of this is triggering the bass' predator instincts. A bass is a hunter, so you must present your fly in such a way that the bass wants to hunt and eat it. This means that if you are retrieving a Swimming Frog you must make it act like a live frog, which will swim for several strokes, pause, and then swim again for several more strokes. Likewise, if you are using a popper painted like a bumblebee, you will get more strikes if you make it act like a bumblebee acts when it finds itself in the water, that being it flutters, spins, and twitches without going very far at all. This action can be imitated by simply shaking your rod tip rapidly back and forth for a few seconds and then pausing and repeating.

Both Steve and Al know that in quiet lily pads, pearl-colored sliders work well. Divers and sliders are bugs with streamlined, down-sloping bodies. Divers dive down a bit when tugged and sliders stay on the surface. I watch minnows. They most often mill about in between or under lily pads, never going too far in one spurt. They frequently turn about, pause, swim a few inches, pause again, turn again, and then repeat the process all day long. By targeting openings in the pads, I can place a slider there and make it appear to be a minnow by changing the angle of my rod tip in relation to my position and the fly, stripping a few inches, and pausing.

You will catch more largemouths if you do not shy away from thick mats of pads and other surface vegetation. Watch such places for swirls and swooshes, then put a large, weedless fly right in the middle of the worst stuff. Twitch the fly right over, around, and through the weeds with a strong leader. When the bass gulps the fly, hesitate for a second or two and then set the hook (which should be long-shanked for increased effectiveness). Under these circumstances, setting the hook the moment the bass strikes will often pull the fly from the outer portions of the fish's mouth before it reaches the back of the mouth.

Where bass are hanging beneath bushes along the shore, try a terrestrial like a Joe's or Dave's Hopper, inchworm imitation, or foam rubber spider. If the bank is grassy, try a Mouserat. Terrestrial insects like grasshoppers, crickets, and inchworms are not strong swimmers, so don't try to make them appear to be something they are not. On the other hand, mice can swim quite well and do so for long stretches without pausing. Retrieve accordingly.

Mid-Range

Between the surface and a few feet below the surface lies an area heavily fly-fished by those who understand that it is where largemouth most often forage. Unfortunately, not enough fly-fishers target bass in this portion of the water column because they don't get to see the vicious attack on the surface, which is part of the draw of bass on the fly.

Bait fish (bream like sunfish and bluegill, and shiners, chubs, trout in some instances, and minnows) and leeches make up the majority of forage eaten by largemouths at mid-range, but larval insects also meet their demise there. By using search patterns, both in the physical sense and by trying different flies, the fly-fisher can determine what looks like a good deal to the bass. In other words, cover as much water as possible while experimenting with assorted flies that mimic different creatures bass may wish to feed on.

Steve and Al use leech imitations on a sink-tip or slow-sinking line a lot of the time because leeches are so common in their region in Minnesota. There, rabbit fur died black or purple is the most popular material because it does an excellent job of imitating the undulating motion of a free-swimming leech. But leeches aren't as common in many other regions of North America, making bait fish flies like streamers very effective. Popular patterns include classics like the Mickey Finn, Carrie Stevens' Gray Ghost, and Muddler Minnow, as well as less well-known

Streamers are often more effective than surface flies.

flies like the Nix's Shinabou. Eel patterns, especially in olive, are also worth a try in the many waters where eels live.

Fly-fishing between the surface and bottom requires you to pay closer attention than when fishing on the surface. Oftentimes the strike is more subtle than one from a surface attack, so one must be alert. Watching and feeling the line at all times will reduce the number of missed fish.

Not being able to see the fly most of the time makes it easy to become lazy. Fly-fishers who focus on presenting the right action all of the time, whether they can see the fly or not, catch more bass. They use continual retrieves when fishing leech patterns, use stop-and-go retrieves when the local bait fish aren't especially nervous or scared, and rapid, darting retrieves when the largemouths are busting shad or shiners.

On or Near the Bottom

Sculpins and crayfish are frequent meals for largemouths prowling along the bottom, and some pretty impressive flies are available that closely mimic them. Good choices include Clousers, Woolhead Sculpins, and Matuka Sculpins.

Fishing a fly along the bottom for largemouths takes even more patience and attention than fishing in the mid-range. The reason lies in how a bass will suck in a crayfish or other prey found on the bottom and *not* turn away, as happens on a surface strike. The bass comes up behind the prey, tips its body downward, and inhales. It then tends to pause rather than rush back to where it came from, and it is this habit that causes so many bass enthusiasts grief.

Although I have no way of telling for sure, I suspect that many fly-fishers targeting the bottom in this way miss more than half of the pick-ups. It is difficult to distinguish between the gentle tap of the bass sucking in the fly and the feel of the fly touching structure. Avoid this problem by keeping tension on the line at all times and always using a sensitive graphite rod that can "telegraph" the strike up the leader and fly line and down the rod to your hands. Never taking your eyes off the line is a big help, too. Another trick, one which tends to bring on more aggressive takes, is to apply some liquid fish attractant to the fly, such as Bait Mate. Ethical? Of course it is, unless, of course, you are a "purist" (one who places restrictions on himself) who frowns on such devious acts. But be warned: The IGFA will disallow any record submission if the fish was caught on a fly with artificial attractant on it.

Another problem is determining what is living on the bottom. For instance, crayfish come in colors ranging from very light green to dark brownish red, and everything in between. This means that bass used to eating dark green crayfish may balk at one that looks out of place. By catching a few crayfish (just turn over some rocks or logs in a foot or two of water to get a look at them) you can solve this glitch.

Be sure to buy or tie crayfish flies that sink quickly to the bottom. Crayfish that seem to float with no visible means will put off larger bass who know something isn't quite right.

To go any further in this chapter would, I fear, turn this book into a largemouth bass fishing book, and that won't do. Let's talk about small-mouths instead.

Smallmouth Bass

Steve Tooker
Steve Tooker Guide Service
Walker, Minnesota

Al Maas
Al Maas Guide Service
Walker, Minnesota

MY YOUTH CONSISTED OF MANY DAYS FISHING MAINE'S LARGELY UNPOPULATED Washington County, which is the easternmost county in America. Made up of evergreen-studded rolling hills adorned with purple carpets of blueberries and their low crimson-leaved bushes, it is home to thundering partridge, tweetering woodcock, stately moose, shy whitetails, and immense numbers of smallmouth bass in lakes that seem absolutely perfect for these marvelous game fish. I would have to say that, given my most treasured memories of high adventure in a boyhood long ago replaced with the trials of screaming jungles, terrible deserts, and distant wars, it is this ancient forest bejeweled with crystalline lakes where one day I will again fish with my grandfather, and his father, too.

Smallmouths evoke passion and inspire all who have cast a fly for them. With their stout bodies of bronze and dark green, they seem to enjoy life to the hilt and imbue in us all the true meanings of happiness, anticipation, and satisfaction.

But why?

Perhaps the answer is *attitude*. Yes, smallmouths have an attitude, one of audacity, tenacity, and a certain relish for aerial antics that make everyone who hooks one on the fly smile.

Native to the eastern half of North America with a stronghold in the Midwest and deep South, the *smallie* or *bronzeback* is a noted fly rod target with which every fly-fisher must become personally involved. Ounce for ounce, the smallmouth puts more *ooomph* into life than the majority of other game fish, fresh and salt alike.

SEASONS AND SIZES

It is interesting to note that nearly all fly rod smallmouth bass records were set in Canada, but that all records set with tackle other than fly were set in the United States, and all but one of those were set in the South.

Smallmouths can grow to weigh more than 10 pounds, but not often. Their habitat dictates how large they will grow (and also the fishing pressure on that habitat), and this can vary radically from water to water, even among waters in the same region. A smallmouth from Maine's Meddybemps Lake will average a little more than a pound—but still fight like a demon—whereas a short ways away in West Grand Lake, a smallmouth will average 2 pounds, maybe more. And a smallmouth from Ontario's Basswood Lake will weigh quite a bit more on the average than both of those lakes, but might have trouble comparing to a smallmouth from Alabama's Pickwick Lake or famous Dale Hollow Reservoir, which is shared by Tennessee and Kentucky.

Likewise, the seasons depend on location, too. In Alabama I can fish for smallies throughout the year, but in north central Minnesota I must get my fishing in between May and very early October while the ice is on vacation.

TACKLE

Smallmouth fly rods include 5- to 8-weight, tip- and mid-flex rods, 8 to 9 feet long. The lighter rods are for pleasant conditions and smaller flies; save the heavier rods for windy days spent tossing wind-resistant deer-hair bugs.

Reels need not be exotic at all. Smallmouths don't peel off hundreds of yards of line, and they don't weigh 100 pounds. A basic reel is all you need, and most of the fish you catch will be handled by stripping them in, although certain waters will see you putting the fish on the reel.

Guides Steve Tooker and Al Maas are very familiar with the seasonal fluctuations of the smallmouth and its habitat; they use everything from full-sink and sink-tip lines to floating lines. By knowing at what depth the smallies will be during each season and at different times within each season, they know what line or lines to take at that time. In the pre-spawn a sink-tip will do nicely to reach the bass on secondary ledges below spawning grounds, and a floating line can be used for smallmouths on the beds. Post-spawn finds fish above the pre-spawn level but below that of the spawn, so either a floating or sink-tip might be called for. Come summer many of the bass move away from the shore and onto mid-lake humps and shoals, but they may be in only 10 to 15 feet of water, so both sink-tips and full-sinks can come in handy. Late in the summer they will find even shallower humps and shoals away from shore, making floating lines worthwhile again, and sometimes sink-tips. As the water begins to cool with the approach of autumn, the smallies go deeper and deeper, so Al and Steve put up the floating lines and go with full-sinks.

Conditions can be different in the South, where winters are less severe and the sun can warm certain areas of the lake so that water temperatures in the shallows get into the low 60s during the afternoon, which smallmouth find pleasant. The trick, as you can see, is to figure out the water. If you know that in the brutal heat of the Alabama summer the smallies will be in the middle of the lake in perhaps 25 feet of water (maybe more), use the fastest sinking line you can find to get down to them, not to mention a short little leader to keep the fly down there near the bottom; perhaps you will even use a weighted fly.

Leaders can be as simple as the reel: 7 1/2- to 10-foot-long tapered leaders (for floating lines) with a butt heavy enough to turn a large popper or deer-hair bug over, between 4- and 8-pound test. Sinking lines need only 3, maybe 4 feet of leader. Sink-tips need 6 to 8 feet or so. You don't have to build your own leader.

Now flies. The selection is staggering because of the very diverse diet of the smallies, which eat darters, crickets, crayfish (number one on many smallmouths' menus), moths, nymphs, worms and nightcrawlers, dace, dragonflies, sculpins, minnows, salamanders, smelt, madtoms, grasshoppers, shad (of critical importance in many Southern waters), alewives, leeches, water dogs, mayflies, shiners, stoneflies, chubs, hellgrammites (which often run a close second to crayfish), caddisflies, and God knows what else. With all these creatures that find their way into the smallmouth's stomach, you can well imagine what a smallmouth fly selection looks like, and yes, it gets ugly.

Rather than list every good smallmouth fly, let me just mention a handful. You'll probably get my drift right away: Muddler Minnows, sculpin imitations, Woolly Buggers, Dahlberg's Crawdad, most deer-hair bugs, Clouser Minnows (outstanding), leech patterns, hellgrammite patterns, dry flies like the Green and Brown Drakes, streamers (especially the Mickey Finn and Gray Ghost), Matukas, hopper imitations (Joe's and Dave's), assorted cork poppers, Madam X, and various wets like the McGinty and Parmacheene Belle. Again, this list could go on for pages, but you get the idea. Start at about size 12 for dry flies, wets, and nymphs, and go as small as a size 18, with sizes 1 to 1/0 or thereabouts for streamers and deer-hair bugs.

TACTICS

Smallmouth tactics for the fly rod are usually simple and direct, using the same formula one would use on dolphin, brown trout, bluefish, coho, pike, and any other fish: Where are the fish, what are they eating (or likely to be eating), and how can I best get at them and present them with a fly they will eat? Answer these questions and you are well on your way.

Photo courtesy of the National Fresh Water Fishing Hall of Fame

Jim Rivers knows how to find big smallies on Alabama's Pickwick Lake.

Where are the fish? A simple question that usually has an equally simple answer. Smallmouths seek water temperatures they feel comfortable in, first of all. Sixty-seven degrees is perfect. It doesn't matter what time of year it is so long as they are comfortable *where they are at the moment.* I am not suggesting that they feel cold or hot—since they are cold blooded they don't. Comfort to them has to do with metabolism: Fish are comfortable when their metabolic functions are normal. They are uncomfortable when their metabolic functions are inefficient, so they relocate. This is one reason smallies move to different parts of a lake or river at different times of the year. Also keep in mind that they may move for a survival reason, such as spawning. However, they will not move into water to feed if the water adversely affects their metabolic rate.

You read in the section about lines how smallmouths move depending on the season and water temperature, and in the spring because they are driven to spawn (almost always in shallows with small rocks, hard, coarse sand, or gravel; reproduction is very poor on soft bottoms of sand, mud, or silt). Once you have found them you can determine what they are eating, if, in fact, they are eating. And even if they aren't feeding at the moment you arrive, there are ways you can make them eat your fly.

The best smallmouth fly-fishers know the forage of the water they are on. In many smallie waters the crayfish is one, if not the most important, forage item, but you must correctly identify the color and size of the crayfish thereabouts. However, there is no need to be able to identify every species of crayfish in North America, of which there are many. Use a crayfish trap or catch some with your hands or a small dip net to quickly determine what crayfish pattern you should use. But don't fall into the habit of assuming there are plenty of crayfish where you are fishing at the moment if you have never fished there before. Crayfish have needs just as bass do, and they prefer rocky areas to those with aquatic vegetation, no matter how sparse, and they prefer rocky areas to those with sand or fine gravel, so be attentive.

This point was driven home a couple of years ago while I was fishing with Al and Steve. We were on a small pond that held both smallies and large-mouths. The shoreline was divided into areas of few weeds with rocks and areas of heavy weeds with no rocks. Every time we approached a rocky area, they would switch flies to a crayfish imitation and catch a smallmouth. When we came up on a weedy area, the crayfish pattern went away and the Dahlberg Diver or Muddler came out, and they would catch a largemouth. *Be attentive* and work your crayfish fly slowly, right on the bottom, with short strips and twitches. If you are really smart, you will use a liquid attractant on your fly that mimics the smell of a crayfish. (Remember, though, that the International Game Fish Association does not recognize fish caught on a fly doused with artificial attractant.)

Another point on crayfish. While fishing Maine's Pocomoonshine Lake in the late 1980s, I was having a dickens of a time producing the number of smallies I had come to expect in that region. Crayfish are an important forage item in that lake and I was casting the biggest crayfish pattern I had. Only one smallie showed up in more than an hour of fishing. Confused, I clipped off the big fly for some unknown reason and tied on one half its size, which was a little over an inch long. The next hour produced 16 smallies. I can't be absolutely certain, but perhaps the reason the smaller fly worked was because smaller crayfish present less of a problem for smallies to catch and eat them. Curious, the following summer I returned to Pocomoonshine at the same time of year (early September) and fished for the first hour with a tiny crayfish pattern that was three-quarters of an inch long. Nothing. I tied on the very same fly that worked so well the previous year and the bass went nuts. I can only guess as to why this was. Maybe the bass didn't feel the small crayfish was worth their effort, or maybe they don't have much luck catching small crayfish that can escape easily by scooting under rocks larger crayfish can't squeeze under.

Smallmouths eat more aquatic insects, especially nymphs, than most anglers realize. In most waters these larval bugs make up at least part of the

Nymphs are more important in many waters than most fly-fishers know. Having the right size is also important. A simple selection, such as these Montana Stonefly nymphs, is sometimes all that is needed.

smallmouth's diet, and in some waters they make up 80 percent of their diet, perhaps more. Maine's St. George River, above Union, is just such a water. There the smallies feast on mayfly and caddisfly nymphs. I have caught bass that were eating so fast and furiously they didn't even wait to swallow before inhaling the next nymph; their mouths were still full of dozens of nymphs when I caught them. Dozens.

Bait fish are also important in many waters. Lakes and reservoirs with substantial populations of small bait fish are more likely to be trophy smallmouth waters than those with crayfish as the primary forage and those with large bait fish like golden shiners. With numerous species of forage fish to prey upon in a single body of water in some cases, it can be tricky deciphering what fly to use to match the bait fish the bass are mostly eating. You have five options:

- Buy some expensive scuba gear and move in with the fish.
- Learn through experience and study what bait fish are most likely to be where and when.
- Use a cast net to capture some bait fish.
- Clean a smallmouth you stumble upon to see what it has been eating.
- Experiment until you come up with a fish.

The method you select will depend on you, but all can work. I've tried them all and found that learning through experience and studying the ecosystem work best most of the time. After that, generally speaking, comes cleaning one that you catch, experimenting, using a cast net, and then scuba. Scuba may seem like the modern, high-tech approach to use.

On more than one occasion I have dived for the sole purpose of finding out what the bass were eating, but one can almost always use other methods. In fact, I recommend you do just that.

Learning about the water you are on is fun and challenging, just like the smallmouth itself. Yes, it takes time, effort, and patience, but it really is the best way to become a better smallmouth specialist.

If you can find smallies and if you have determined what they are eating, the next part usually comes easy. Getting at them and presenting them a fly they find worth eating is a matter of having the right tackle and knowing how to use it. Assuming you have the right tackle—especially the right line and length leader—let's look at the presentation by examining the smallmouth's senses.

I have suggested dousing your fly with attractant. This can work well, but you are dealing with a species that has only a mediocre sense of smell. Therefore, you must use the right attractant under the right conditions. This means using crayfish attractant in a crayfish area under conditions that lend themselves to its use. Such conditions are reduced visibility and increased turbidity, preferably both at the same time. Why these conditions? Because smallmouths have better hearing and a more finely tuned lateral line than they do a sense of smell. In cloudy, moving water they will use their sense of smell to help make up for their reduced ability to pick up vibrations and sounds from nearby prey. But you must also consider the fish's eyesight, which in daylight hours is generally very good. So, if you use a fly that is pretty visible and smells good, all the better.

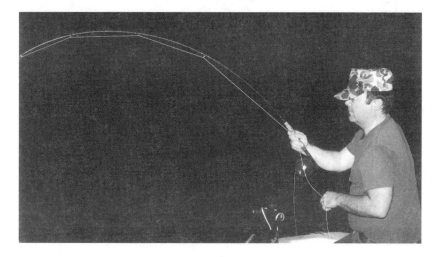

When fishing at night, the smallmouth's hearing is often the sense to exploit.

Of the bronzeback's four senses, its daytime vision is by far the sharpest (but its nighttime vision is average, at best). Because of this, the smallmouth hunts using its sight more than hearing, smell, and vibrations (detected by the bass' lateral line). This knowledge may be the fly-fisher's most valuable asset, because once you know *how* the fish prefers to hunt, all other information becomes somewhat less of a concern. All in all, if he can't see it, he can't eat it. This is an important point, for now you are probably thinking—and correctly so—that smallmouths prefer water with at least fair visibility. This is why lakes and rivers with consistently poor visibility are never good smallmouth habitats. But there is a caveat to this visibility rule. Smallmouths are somewhat sensitive to light and prefer cloud cover to bright sunshine. When the clouds move in, the fish will move to shallower water and start to hunt aggressively, particularly in clear-water lakes. (And night fishing in these clear lakes is often better than night fishing in murky lakes.)

If you are after the very biggest of smallies, look for rocky or gravelly waters with little fishing pressure where there are excellent numbers of smaller bait fish. A lake or reservoir with these attributes that has a terraced bottom (areas that are flat) and high average temperatures in the upper 60s is a prime candidate. And if the smallies aren't forced to compete with other predators like northern pike and largemouth bass, all the better.

Smaller bait fish in large numbers are often a crucial part of the trophy smallmouth equation.

The best rivers for smallmouths are those with reasonable visibility and current that is moderate—not too slow and not too fast. The bottom must have rocks and gravel, or at least coarse, hard sand, and there must be sufficient prey with, hopefully, minimal competition from other game fish.

Pike are next on the docket.

5

Northern Pike

Brian and Sharon Elder
Wollaston Lake Lodge
Saskatchewan, Canada

Steve Tooker
Steve Tooker Guide Service
Walker, Minnesota

Al Maas
Al Maas Guide Service
Walker, Minnesota

YOU MET STEVE TOOKER AND AL MAAS IN CHAPTERS 3 (LARGEMOUTH BASS) AND 4 (smallmouth bass), so you know they are well qualified to speak on fishing for anything else that swims in their waters, which includes a great many northern pike. I've spent quite a few hours with Steve and Al hunting for trophy pike on fabled lakes such as Leech Lake in north central Minnesota, and they have taught me much of what I know about fly-fishing for pike. Of course, they are so far ahead of me in pike wisdom that I may never catch up, but every summer I still try to close the gap when we meet on cold waters amid an emerald forest, far from my home in the Rockies.

SEASONS AND SIZES

One reason northern pike are so popular with fly-fishers is that they are available right after ice-out through autumn and even, in their extreme southernmost range, during the winter in some places. But pike fanatics know the best pike fishing is in the colder climes. This is because the northern pike lives much longer in the northland, prowling the cabbage beds (broad-leaved pondweed) and breaklines for up to 25 years and then some; in more southerly waters pike only average about 6 years of life and therefore never have a chance to reach genuine maturity.

According to Steve and Al, late spring sees excellent pike action as the fish move up into the shallows to spawn, but by mid-July the larger fish become less aggressive on the whole and stay that way until autumn when the pike seem to go crazy, attacking a wide array of flies in somewhat deeper water (many of their favorite shallow weed beds die off in the fall, so the fish seek structure in deeper water where many species of aquatic vegetation remain vital for up to a month after the shallow-water plants have "turned"). Of course, they admit that the juvenile pike (called "hammer-handles" in these parts) can be easily taken on flies all summer long, especially in the mornings and evenings (the fishing definitely falls off come mid-day). Both guides stress that water temperature is very important, with prime feeding temperature being in the mid-60s. Once the water temperature starts getting into the lower- to mid-70s, pike like to take a snooze.

In pike country, Steve and Al say a good pike starts at about 10 pounds or so, but if you like a thrill, the single-digit pike can really be fun when taken on a fly rod meant for trout, such as a 7 1/2-foot, full-flex, 6-weight rod. They stress, however, that if you are going to use such flimsy tackle and still want to release the pike safely, you need to always use a heavy enough leader and tippet so that you can put the pressure on the fish and play it quickly.

TACKLE

You shouldn't be equipped with anything less than an 8 1/2-foot, mid-flex, 8-weight rod. A 9-foot, 9-weight is even better, since big pike like big flies, and casting those big flies into a breeze requires power. (An efficient casting technique works wonders, too.)

Weight-forward, floating, or sink-tip lines are what you need most of the time, as the majority of strikes come from fish that see the fly above their ambush position in the weeds. When the weeds are just below the surface, use the floating line, and when they are several feet down, you may find that a sink-tip is more effective in getting the fly farther into the strike zone. However, pike have excellent senses, including a lateral line that helps them sense prey nearby, and sensitive pores along their body that add to their hunting prowess. This means that the strike zone, depending on the conditions, can be quite large. (Steve, Al, and I have seen pike come charging from as far as 30 feet away to get at a fly they wanted.)

Come mid-summer when the water is at its warmest, the pike may suspend a little deeper, requiring you to use a full-sink line. This is the time to tie on the biggest, gaudiest white Dahlberg Diver you have, preferably one with some Flashabou to reflect as much light as possible. Let the line pull it all the way down until the fly is floating just above the weeds, then strip the fly in with quick dashes and a pause after every third or fourth dash. Be very ready when you begin to strip after the pause.

Flies run the gamut. While Whistlers, Sea-Ducers, and many styles of flies made from rabbit fur are popular and productive, we have been experimenting with other saltwater flies like those that imitate menhaden. I have found the best to be Curcione's Big Game Fly and Peterson's Giant Bunker, two flies known more for taking little tunny, bluefish, and stripers than for taking pike. Large pencil poppers are also excellent.

Remember that because northern pike are so big, strong, and toothy, you are going to need some special items.

Wire leaders are required for the biggest pike, and naturally this means that you will want a pair of long hook removers, which will be even more effective if you use a jaw spreader.

The standard round net is no good for big pike, since it can easily hurt them as they thrash about in the net. Use a cradle instead, which secures the fish nicely and allows you to release it with less risk of injury to the fish.

Expect your flies to get torn up quickly; have plenty along. And that armored maw means you will need a hook file or other sharpener handy to make your hooks their sharpest.

A few absorbent rags are a must, since pike are slimy. However, do not wrap the fish in the rag. The rag is for wiping your hands; it will strip a pike's slime if you use it to grasp the fish, and this substantially reduces the fish's chance of survival after release.

TACTICS

Your pike fly-fishing tactics will be more effective if you first find a lake that pike thrive in. Such lakes are fairly fertile, with a nice mixture of assorted favored weeds and rocks, varying depths (although the 20-foot mark is about as deep as pike like to go), and plenty of bait fish like suckers, perch, ciscoes, bass, and sunfish. The lake also should maintain plenty of water that can hold for longer periods in the mid-60s. Waters that are overgrown with weeds (very fertile lakes, which tend to be too warm to support a prime pike population) or too rocky and infertile can hold pike, but trophy fish will be rare. Lakes like Wollaston are perfect.

Rivers that hold the best pike action have the same attributes as the best pike lakes, but avoid rivers with lots of fast-moving water and no quiet backwaters and eddies for the pike to hide in. Fly-fishing for pike can be ridiculously easy to maddeningly difficult—and everything in between—all in a single day's fishing. I believe that pike are affected by tiny changes in the weather and water conditions more than most freshwater fish, because of how often I see the fishing go from one extreme to the other. That said, I have found that when the fish suddenly turn off in one area, such as after a feeding frenzy immediately before and during a cold snap (pike love to feed heavily as a cold front moves in and will continue to dine until the front starts moving out), you shouldn't automatically think the entire lake has gone dead. Instead of heading back to the dock, try other patches of likely looking water that aren't being worked at the moment. Switch flies and presentations as well, and be especially watchful of the smaller spots that may

This pike was taken from a cabbage patch in less than 10 feet of water.

hold a pike or two. Check holes in thick milfoil, cabbage (broad-leaved pondweeds are far more productive than narrow-leaved), and coontail. In areas where walleye and yellow perch may be holding just off a bed of bulrushes, try a Mickey Finn or green and yellow Deceiver or Clouser. And around the largest lily pads you can find, toss a hefty deer-hair bug or big saltwater-style popper like those used for redfish on the spartina flats around Charleston.

Although pike don't have a well-developed sense of smell, they do use it to hunt when their other senses are less effective. I have had excellent success time and again during spring and fall, when the water is cold and visibility is poor, by using some scent on my flies. I'll soak a streamer with an attractant (I have yet to determine if one flavor is better than another) and dead-drift the fly over a weed bed. This technique works, even though some people will tell you that pike never hunt by smell.

One of the most unnerving and evil things a pike will do to you—and they tend to do it often and seem to really enjoy it—is follow your fly right up to the boat in plain view, or hide beneath the boat and strike viciously just as you start to pick the line up. When the pike is tormenting you by lollygagging along right behind your fly, try this trick: Softly lower the rod's tip into the water until it is 3 or 4 feet below the boat. Keeping the fly line pinched against the cork, work the rod in as wide a figure-8 pattern as you can. Pike often strike when they see the "fish" they are chasing change direction again and again. When the pike hits, <u>do not</u> set the hook immediately, as this will often yank the fly right out of its mouth. Instead, set the hook by twisting your body sideways only when you actually feel the weight of the fish as it turns away with the fly in its mouth. Be prepared to let the fish take the line once the hook is set, and make sure it isn't tangled around something in the boat, like your foot, trolling motor, Labrador, or daughter. (Bad show, that.)

Pay close attention to water clarity. Pike see fairly well in clear water, and they often spook if they see you,

Feeding frenzies sometimes include other pike as prey, as the scars on this pike attest.

especially trophy fish that have learned to identify the human silhouette with danger. Juvenile fish may not spook as easily.

Check to see what bait fish are nearby and try to match them with a fly of the same color and size. If this fails, tie on a much larger fly of the same color. No good? Wake them up with a vigorous retrieve of a noisy deer-hair bug or pencil popper. Still nothing doing? Tie some Flashabou into the fly and throw it at them.

For some of the biggest pike on the continent, go to Wollaston Lake Lodge. There are huge, mean pike here and lots of them. Pike deserve your respect and attention. Go give them some of both.

6 Rainbow and Brown Trout

Jennifer and Lars Olsson
Professional Guides
Bozeman, Montana

Mickey and Maggie Greenwood
Blackfire Flyfishing Guest Ranch
Angel Fire, New Mexico

I COVER RAINBOWS AND BROWNS TOGETHER IN A SINGLE CHAPTER BECAUSE, although they are taxonomically two completely different species, fly-fishing for one is usually very similar—though not always in results achieved—to fly-fishing for the other. They often live in the very same body of water, be it a stream, river, lake, pond, or reservoir, and they feed on the same forage, be it insects, bait fish, or crustaceans. They use the same lies and have similar needs in water quality and temperature, although the rainbow is more hearty when it comes to water in which it can inhabit and reproduce. But there is one clear difference between the two trout besides their being different fish: The brown trout isn't from North America, and the rainbow trout is.

Yes, the brown is a foreigner.

But before we discuss how the brown came to be in North American waters, first a note on the rainbow's confused lineage.

As you will learn in Chapter 12, steelhead are anadromous rainbow trout. But wait. About 10 years ago some sticklers for minutiae got together to talk about the rainbow trout and its allegedly anadromous form, the steelhead. These people were the American Society of Ichthyologists and Herpetologists Committee on Names of Fishes (come on, you knew *someone* had to name the fishes).

These folks decided, after reviewing all the available evidence, that we had it backwards. You see, the steelhead isn't an anadromous rainbow trout after all, and the rainbow trout isn't a trout, either. In reality, the rainbow trout is a landlocked steelhead, and a steelhead isn't a trout but a Pacific salmon, related to the chinook, sockeye, and the rest of the gang. Therefore, the scientists took the rainbow trout, er, salmon, out of its previous genus (*Salmo*) and released it into the genus of the Pacific salmon (*Oncorhynchus*). Then they changed its species to *mykiss*, making the fish *Oncorhynchus mykiss*.

Understand? Good.

(Actually, like most of the things I know about fly-fishing—which some acquaintances of mine say really isn't all that much—I learned of this rainbow trout–salmon debacle from another fly-fisher, Silvio Calabi, who edits *Fly Rod & Reel*, a magazine owned by Down East Enterprises, which owns Down East Books, who published one of my first books, *The Complete Guide to Fly Fishing Maine*. I'm telling you this because I can't stand it when a fly-fisher seems to pretend or insinuate that he or she is the original source of some piece of fly-fishing knowledge when, in reality, he or she is anything but. Truth is, totally original thinkers are a rare commodity, and the genuine article, like Lee Wulff and Nick Lyons, are rare specimens whom I dare not even fantasize about being lumped in with some day, long after I have left this planet.

But as of late the rainbow has acquired more than just an identity crisis.

Whirling disease, a crippling malady transmitted by a parasite that found its way into hatcheries, is now considered a major threat to the health of Western rainbow trout. The disease has also spread east, and browns and brookies also have been found to be susceptible, though not to the degree rainbows are. As of this writing, whirling disease is a serious ailment that we have yet to get a handle on.

A classic Colorado River brown

All that aside—yeah, as if we are going to now call the rainbow *trout* the rainbow *salmon*—let's get back to the brown trout and how it slipped by the Immigration and Naturalization Service.

The brown trout first came to America from Germany in 1884, having been released into Michigan's Pere Marquette River. They survived and thrived. A year later, another batch of browns, these from Scotland's Loch Leven in Kinross, were brought to America and they, too, did very well. (These Loch Leven browns are known for their dark spots and lack of red spots.)

Decades passed. The two strains of browns, one from German rivers and streams, the other from a big (3,500 acres), cold lake in Scotland situated between the Firth of Forth and the Earn, spread and began to eventually mix. Soon, America had her own brown trout, and it would be one of the most discerning trout to ever swim in North America, known to refuse the very best presentation of a flawless fly, even when the rainbows, cutthroats, and brookies are feeding with abandon.

This isn't surprising. Take the adaptability of the German and toss in the individuality of the Scot, mix the result with the eclectic appetite of the German and add the discriminating taste of the Scot, and you get the American brown trout.

SEASONS AND SIZES

Both browns and rainbows can be found from coast to coast, from The Forks on the Kennebec to many streams in northern California, and both species have been successfully stocked in the Southeast, creating what may be an unexpected fishery for some in the southernmost Appalachians. Given this wide range, check the seasons for each state. Keep in mind, too, that "season" also means what insects are hatching. This can get pretty technical; guides like Jennifer and Lars Olsson have to know these specifics or else they go hungry.

Jennifer and Lars guide on Montana rivers like the Yellowstone, Gallatin, and Madison, and on spring creeks like DePuy's, Nelson's, and O'Hair's. They begin their year in mid-March and fish the rivers until the run-off in mid-May. Little Olives undergo spectacular hatches during this time (with a good caddis hatch around Mother's Day), but in the fall the big hatches are Tiny Blue Quills.

The sizes of browns and rainbows are equally diverse. While a 10-inch trout is considered a dandy in nearly all Blue Mountain streams in Appalachia, a trout of the same size caught on the Bighorn is considered an embarrassing fluke by many snobbish fly-fishers who fish only for the largest specimens rather than for the experience of interacting with nature.

TACKLE

Some research is called for then—before you get on the plane—to determine when you should go where and what tackle you should take. I learned a couple of lessons at Mickey and Maggie Greenwood's Blackfire

Flyfishing Guest Ranch in northern New Mexico's Sangre de Cristo Mountains late in the summer of 1997. Their trout pond is jammed with giant rainbows (and some scary cutts, too), with the rainbows averaging 4–8 pounds. These are big, healthy fish that fight like demons. I broke two off using a 5X tippet and soon went heavier. Knowing that the pond was filled with these brutes, I quickly realized that I would continue to lose fish if I didn't up the ante just a bit.

I caught my first brown on Maine's North Pond within sight of tourist-crammed Route 1 in Warren. This was about 1969 as best I can recall, and I was fly-fishing with my father for bass. It was early June and the bass were on the beds.

Poppers were in order, and I had tied on my favorite bass bug, a fly I had purchased two years earlier at Eckerd Drugs in Sunrise, Florida, which back then was a sprawling subdivision near Plantation called Sunrise Golf

Pete Deison with a classic Blackfire rainbow.

Village. The fly was called the Playboy popper. It was a typical bass bug, painted mostly white with a couple of black stripes and a few black and white feathers sticking out the back end. I bought it not for the pattern but for the name, as I was keenly interested in the anatomical research magazine of the same name at that point in my life (I was 9 years old). I assumed that, with such a name, the fly would catch great hoards of fish. I was precisely correct in my assumption, as it delivered hundreds of Maine smallmouths before it finally fell apart after a fine fight with a smallie on Washington County's Crawford Lake.

The trout smacked the bug after two twitches and I thought it looked different than the bass we had been taking. About a minute later my father netted the fish and, sure enough, it looked quite different from the bass. I ate it for supper.

That first brown—caught one year after my first brookie—taught me an important lesson about browns: They eat more than just mayflies, midges, and caddis, and they can handily be caught with a 7-weight, 8 1/2–foot rod.

But that particular rod wouldn't be right for sea-run browns in the Ogunquit River along the Maine coast in February. Yes, sea-run versions of browns can be caught not only in select streams and rivers in North America, but also from the British Isles (as you might expect) to Patagonia (southern Argentina is known for the finest sea-run brown fishing anywhere). That rod wouldn't be right on Colorado's St. Vrain or on Redington Pond in the Redington Pond Range in Maine, where the smallish browns are best caught with a 4-weight or so, although I have seen some monstrous browns come out of remote Redington Pond (the headwaters of Orbeton Stream), a pond known more for excellent brookie fishing. And that rod would be a bit heavy for catching browns in the Cherokee Nation's ponds and streams in North Carolina.

And the same goes for rainbows.

So again, homework is called for. Still, if I had to pick one rod to use on browns and rainbows across North America, I would select a mid-flex 6-weight between 8 1/2 and 9 feet.

Perhaps the specifics of the reel are somewhat more important than those of the rod when it comes to big browns and 'bows. For instance, I have taken some fine rainbows (hatchery fish) from Lake Cuyamaca in the mountains above San Diego, trout that had become smart and had grown to a few pounds. The reel I used was an inexpensive but acceptable reel for handling fish of that size. However, had I found myself fighting one of the lake's 9-pound rainbows, I wonder if the reel's drag—which I had seldom put to the test—would have survived. Along the same lines, hefty rainbows in fast water will often test a drag's mettle, with the added stress of the moving water to determine whether the reel is right or wrong. Therefore, if you will be fishing on water with big trout, especially if that water is a powerful river, never shortchange yourself on the reel you select.

Lines cover the spectrum. In Colorado's high-country lakes, full-sinks and sink-tips are the norm when casting big black Woolly Buggers, but floating lines are needed for much of the fishing on Colorado's rivers. Check the conditions before you leave, no matter where you are going.

Leaders used with dry flies for browns and rainbows are often quite long. They might also be quite fine with a tippet section that looks and feels more like a mist web than a piece of monofilament. This is because rainbows and especially browns can become extremely line shy. This tendency gave birth to the phrase "I lined him," which refers to the trout being scared away by a line hitting the surface or a line simply being seen by a spooky trout.

Tom Rosenbauer, in his foundational book, *The Orvis Fly-Fishing Guide*, describes building a standard trout leader to use for casting average-sized flies (sizes 12–16) on typical mid-season water.

He starts with a bit more than a 36-inch butt, .021 in diameter, and ties a 16-inch piece of .019 to that. This is followed by a 12-inch piece of .017, to complete the butt section. The midsection of the leader consists of four 6-inch pieces of .015, .013, .011, and finally .009. The tippet is 20 inches of 4X (.007) which rates to just over 3 pounds tensile strength. To tie all these mono sections together, use a surgeon's knot (my first recommendation) or a barrel knot.

Leaders really aren't difficult to build, and once you are truly addicted to catching paranoid trout you probably will want to always use your own leaders. But for out-of-the-package leaders, Jennifer and Lars recommend a 9-foot, 3X–7X for dry flies, wets, and nymphs, unless it is a windless, bright sunny day and you have a flat surface, which calls for a 12-foot leader. If you are using a weighted nymph, split shot, and a strike indicator, or are deep nymphing, they suggest a 2X–5X, 7 1/2–foot leader. (They prefer Climax leaders for their 25% stiff butt and 25% soft tip with a middle section that continues the turnover well.) When using full-sinks or sink-tips, the guides say to use a leader between 3 and 5 feet long.

Flies for rainbows and browns are perhaps the most diverse of all types of fly-fishing. Dries, wets, nymphs, terrestrials, and streamers are all effective if properly presented under the right conditions. So what do you do? Head for your local fly shop and buy half a dozen of every fly in every size? No. You learn about the water you will be on and the conditions you will be fishing under before you arrive at streamside (or lakeside), and have what you need when you get there by either buying or tying at home or buying at the local fly shop.

Knowing what to have with you means more trout for you. When Jennifer and Lars are fishing around Mother's Day, they carry Squirrel Caddis, Elk Hair Caddis, and Quill-wing Caddis; green, brown, and tan caddis worms; and winged March Browns. They also carry a midge pupa pattern called the Serendipity, developed by Dave and Lynn Corcoran, owners of the River's Edge Fly Shop in Bozeman. With a body of twisted antron yarn and a head of either deer or caribou hair, the Olssons swear by this little fly. A size 20, dark brown Serendipity has produced 20-inch browns and rainbows for Jennifer.

The salmonfly hatch in the Olsson's region happens toward the end of the runoff. Salmonflies are actually giant stoneflies that can have

*Harriet Deison works
a bead-head Gold-ribbed Hare's Ear
in northern New Mexico's Sangre de Cristo Mountains.*

wingspans of 4 inches and bodies of 2 inches. This is a dramatic hatch that, as Jennifer puts it, "makes the streamside banks look like they are moving."

The end of and following the salmonfly hatch see two very important mayfly hatches that Jennifer and Lars exploit: Pale Morning Duns and Western Green Drakes. Then they get ready for the summer fishery and focus on those tiny Tricos, as well as terrestrials blown into the water from the surrounding grasslands. Also during the summer, evening hatches that start at about 6 P.M. can be incredible, with mayflies and caddis in swarms. Says Jennifer: "Watch the hatch, use an insect net, match the hatch, look for hatching duns and falls of spinners and caddis, copy the size, shape, and color!" That's all there is to it.

I'm going to go out on a limb here—not a good place to be because wise guy fly-fishers, who actually *do* know everything there is to know about fly-fishing and take great pleasure in pointing it out at inopportune moments, like to saw the branch off—and list a very general selection of flies for browns and rainbows. Bear in mind, however, that a certain fly (or size of a certain fly) on one water may be useless at any given time on another. These flies vary in size, too.

Dries: Adams, Green Drake, Brown Drake, Light and Dark Hendricksons, Royal Wulff, assorted spinners (spinners are sexually mature mayflies), assorted Comparaduns, Light Cahill, Blue Quill, Royal Coachman, March Brown, Blue Dun, Humpy (red, white, green, and yellow), Quill Gordon, Mosquito, and assorted Tricos.

Wets: March Brown, Quill Gordon, Adams, Hornberg, Light Cahill, Parmacheene Belle, and Royal Coachman.

Nymphs (weighted and not): Brassie, Gold-ribbed Hare's Ear, Prince, Zug Bug, Scud (assorted colors), Montana Stone, Bead Head Caddis, Golden Stone, Disco Midge, Hendrickson, Pheasant Tail, and Telico.

Terrestrials: Whitlock's Hopper, Dave's Hopper, Joe's Hopper, assorted ant patterns, assorted beetle patterns, and Dave's Inchworm.

Streamers: All the Ghosts (Black, Gray, Green, and Red), Kennebago Smelt, assorted Muddlers (a new take on that design appears approximately every two seconds), Woolly Buggers (black and olive), Black-nose Dace, Mickey Finn, and the Nine-Three.

Finally, in streams and rivers where salmon spawn, egg patterns are a must.

Mark Rayman of the St. Vrain Angler Fly Shop in Longmont, Colorado, understands the importance of reading the water, as this fine brown demonstrates.

TACTICS

Tactics for browns and rainbows living in rivers and streams revolve around energy, i.e., flow of the water and how it affects your fly's drift. If you can use or circumvent the water's ability to place drag on the fly and therefore make it appear suspicious, you have won half the game. (The second half is, of course, matching the hatch.) In lakes, ponds, and reservoirs, it can also be matching the hatch, but there it is more often determining what forage fish, crustaceans, and other edibles are swimming around down there, and then imitating them.

Jennifer and Lars lay it out for us:

"When dry fly-fishing, it is necessary to achieve a drag-free drift. Some of our naturals move on the surface or are being blown by the wind across part of the stream, but they <u>never</u> move on the water like a dry fly tied onto a leader does. An occasional lift of the rod tip, a pull with the hand, or a twitch, will move the fly enough to sometimes fool a trout. Caddis move like that on the water when hatching, and both stoneflies and caddis do when laying eggs.

"There are several slack line and leader casts that make for good presentations, like the parachute cast, bounce cast, serpentine cast, and reach cast."

Line control plays an equally important role in fishing wets and nymphs.

Jan Purdy has also mastered the art and science of reading the water.

"Just like dry fly-fishing," the guides point out, "the nymph and the wet fly, fished in the film or a few inches under, can be presented and fished in the same way, drag-free or with a slight 'dragging'/swimming motion. When fishing across or downstream, the fly can move without drag, or swim in the right way, if you mend the line correctly. We fish a lot downstream using the wet-fly swing technique, keeping the rod tip high and mending the line when necessary."

It can be tricky at first to learn how to fish a weighted nymph on an upstream presentation, but Jennifer and Lars cut through the murk.

"The biggest mistake a fly-fisherman can make when fishing a heavy nymph with or without split shots upstream (or quartering) is to cast too far. The short leader and short line will make for a better presentation and form an almost straight line to the fly. The current will pull the line just enough so that the strike is detected, that is, the strike indicator stops or moves upstream."

Now you can see how this is a science of physics and physiology—energy and how living things function.

It helps to think like a trout: Where can I position myself so that food comes to me, I can identify it and eat it easily with minimal effort, and I am protected from my enemies?

Such a place is a lie, which is formed by some structure or other feature (a depression or eddy, for instance) of the stream that reduces the flow a trout faces. Even the

Mark Waldron read the water and came up with this beautiful rainbow.

slightest depression, the smallest eddy, and the most obscure rock or branch can afford the trout a place to eat safely and efficiently. Learn to "read the water."

Reading the water takes time, attention to detail, deduction, and a knowledge of the trout's habits. Although you don't have to start with a good book on the subject, I find that reading—having some advance knowledge of the subject before beginning the practical application phase—helps me imagine and grasp concepts. Start with *Fly Fishing Basics* by Dave Hughes (available from Stackpole Books). Read it through and then begin your training streamside with a knowledgeable fly-fisher who is willing to teach you. Experiment. Fish as often as possible. Watch the water. You'll learn.

But reading the water in trout ponds can be quite different. At Blackfire Flyfishing Guest Ranch in New Mexico, it is commonplace to sight-fish for the prowling trophy rainbows that cruise the shoreline. In ponds you often find the trout coming to the fly instead of the fly going to the trout, as happens in a stream. But just because trout are in a pond doesn't mean that they are easy marks, because they tend to get smarter as the summer progresses. They recognize flies that have fooled them before and shy away.

Nevertheless, old stand-bys like nymphs, the appropriate dry fly during a *Callibaetis* or caddis hatch, and wets that can mimic emergers will fool these rascals. But as Mickey pointed out, it is important in this situation to fish slowly, allowing the trout time to reach and examine the fly you are offering. Competition may not be especially fierce, even in a small pond with big fish, because there could easily be plenty of forage available. Think and fish logically.

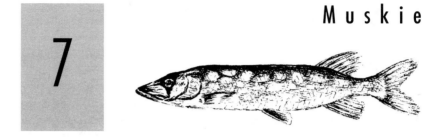

Steve Tooker
Steve Tooker Guide Service
Walker, Minnesota

Al Maas
Al Maas Guide Service
Walker, Minnesota

OF GAME FISH CONSIDERED TOUGH TO TAKE ON A FLY IN NORTH AMERICA, THE muskie rates right up there among the obscenely difficult. With this gauntlet thrown down, we are fortunate to have two of North America's top muskie experts, Steve Tooker and Al Maas, to tell us how to beat the odds and beat this outrageous game fish with the long rod.

The muskellunge, a.k.a. *muskie, musky,* and *keep-your-hands-away-from-its-mouth,* is one of the most coveted game fish in the world. Growing to nearly 70 pounds of Machiavellian cunning and guile, the muskie, which comes in barred, spotted, and plain color patterns, amounts to a freshwater version of a great barracuda, and it has many of the same attributes to boot. When it hits, it hits hard. It is evil. It jumps and thrashes wildly. It is evil. It has the startling habit of attacking the fly right at the side of the boat. It is evil. It wrecks your tackle. It is evil.

And it is evil.

SEASONS AND SIZES

Although muskie are fish of colder waters, they have been transplanted in the South with some success. But the best muskie fishing is in the North; states like Minnesota and Wisconsin are known for great fishing, and provinces like Quebec and Ontario are equally outstanding, sometimes more so.

With such a northerly orientation, muskie are fish of late spring, summer, and early fall, with the best action coming in June and September. Strangely, juvenile muskie aren't nearly as often caught as, say, juvenile barracuda. When you hit a muskie, it stands a good chance of being a big one, weighing well into the 20s and likely into the 30s.

TACKLE

Fly tackle for muskie means long, heavy rods, big reels, and big flies tied to a wire leader or very heavy mono tippet (often 50- to 80-pound test).

The rod should be absolutely no less than a tip-flex 9-weight, 9-feet long or more. It is better still to go with something between a 10- and 12-weight for the biggest fish. Make no mistake here: These brutes are, well, *brutes*. If you are casting flies for bass or average pike and an average muskie hits it, you have a real problem.

Reels must be superior, with the best drags. Lots of line capacity is a prerequisite. Big Abel, Penn, Sage, Orvis, or like models are needed.

Fly lines for muskie include weight-forward floating, sink-tips, and full-sinks. Intermediate lines can be useful as well. On windy days (or not so windy days) a shooting head can be a godsend.

Leaders have to be strong and resilient. A 10-foot leader in the 20- to 30-pound class is standard, with tippets being wire (30- to 50-pound class) or very heavy mono up to 80-pound test. (Muskie have very sharp, very big teeth so the wrong leader or tippet won't last long.) The butt section of a muskie leader attached to a floating line should be 5 or 6 feet long, half that when used with a sinking line or sink-tip. Wire tippets made of coated nylon should be 12 to 16 inches.

Now, flies are a science unto their own. Two years ago Steve and Al asked me to send them some big game saltwater flies like those used for sailfish, marlins, and tuna. I sent them up from my home on the coast and they put the flies to work on the muskie. I mean *big* flies like Curcione's tandem Big Game Fly and a favorite striper fly of mine, Peterson's Giant Bunker, plus Sea-Ducers, Whistlers, and Stu Apte's Tarpon Fly as big as 4/0. Flashabou in muskie flies is a plus, and weighted flies made from rabbit fur are also productive, but make them plenty long (8 to 16 inches).

Muskie fishing with flies isn't that expensive a proposition since, unlike barracuda, it often takes a thousand casts to get a strike. Even the most serious muskie fly-fishers land only a handful of these beasts every year.

You will also need all the support gear (jaw spreaders, hook removers, and so on) needed for pike (as discussed in Chapter 5).

TACTICS

Muskie tactics are more specific than those employed against their little cousin, the northern pike. Where generalities are broadly applied with pike, this isn't always the case with muskie. For instance, two years ago Steve and I took off from his marina on Minnesota's Leech Lake (he owns and operates Loe's Resort on the big lake). It was early afternoon, and we sped past quite a few beds of cabbage and coontail that looked pretty good to me. We continued on for another 10 minutes at full throttle (on Steve's water rocket that works out to about 400 MPH) until finally I detected several boats sitting on the pan-flat surface about a mile away. We pulled in near them.

We stopped over a submerged cabbage patch in about 10 feet of water. I asked Steve why we had run all this way (several miles) when we could have simply stopped at one of the other similar-looking cabbage beds we had passed along the way.

"Well," Steve replied with a matter-of-fact Minnesota accent, "we didn't stop at those ones because there aren't any muskie on them."

Ohhhhhhhhkay.

Steve has a way with words, and few of them at that.

Come to find out, muskie have definite preferences when it comes to structure, and although one kind of structure looks just like another to the untrained human eye, this isn't the case with the muskie's eye. It knows what it wants, and what it wants is just the right cover with just the right type and amount of forage. If a cabbage bed, log, or coontail patch doesn't fit the mold, the muskie won't live there.

So muskie fishing is a game of knowing what local haunts hold muskie, not just knowing what local haunts *look* like they might hold muskie.

An important consideration, according to Al, is the availability of large bait fish like suckers. But Al also notes that if the bait fish on a certain piece of structure average 8 inches, then you should cast flies that mimic not only their species but also their size. And in the spring, Al and Steve say, sometimes smaller flies in general are better. The same applies to weather conditions that tend to put the muskie down, like fast-moving cold fronts.

Further, if the muskie are hitting short, switch to a tandem fly. (Muskie are notorious for "boiling" short of the forward-set hook on a fly.)

Fly-fishing at night for trophy muskie is becoming more popular on warm summer nights, especially just before a thunderstorm. The muskie move into the shallows in such situations; don't hesitate to cast flies (big noisy ones) into water

Al Maas hoists a typical Minnesota muskie.

three feet deep or even less. Fish quietly and listen for the sounds of muskie feeding. Cast your fly there and wait until your rod bends under the weight of the muskie before you set the hook with a full waist twist to the side.

Check the water clarity. Lakes with frequently clear water, like Leech Lake, have the best muskie action early and late in the day because visibility is good. But on lakes with cloudy water, muskie will frequently become active at midday while the sun is high in the sky and the light can penetrate better.

Don't automatically pass up rocks and logs in favor of pondweed and coontail. Sometimes muskie hold on thinner cover.

If you live in a region where reservoirs are common and there are muskie in them, such as where I live in Colorado (I fish for tiger muskie, a muskie/pike hybrid on Quincy Reservoir and Williams Fork Reservoir), your tactics will need a little refinement. The key is paying close attention to how the water level is changing. If the water is rising, start casting toward shore to entice the muskie moving into the new water and new structure that was inaccessible a little while ago. Conversely, in water that is falling, start heading out into deeper water, and remember that muskie are very picky about depth; a slight change might be all the impetus they need to relocate.

Although you will make many casts to even interest a muskie in most situations, they are certainly worth your time and effort. The thrill of catching one on the fly evens the score.

Time for my favorite trout—well, char. The brook trout is up next.

8

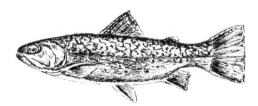

Brook Trout

Joe Stefanski
Diana Lake Lodge
Kuujjuaq, Quebec, Canada
and
Lake Ternay Lodge
Quebec, Canada

BROOK TROUT HAVE BEEN CALLED "JEWEL-LIKE" BY SILVIO CALABI, AND I SUSPECT that other authors before them have used similar geological metaphors to describe this wonderful char. Yes, like the rainbow trout is apparently a salmon, the beautiful brook trout is in fact a char, related to lake trout, arctic char, Dolly Varden, and two of the rarest char, the blueback trout (found in Maine's Floods Pond) and the Sunapee trout (which takes its name from the lake in New Hampshire, hence the uppercasing of Sunapee). (Both the Sunapee and blueback are believed by some to be landlocked arctic char, so you can see how taxonomic classification isn't quite a perfect process.)

The brookie is a special game fish. Very intolerant of anything but the purest water (and preferring temperatures in the low- to mid-60s and tolerating a maximum of about 75 degrees), yet prone to overpopulation and sometimes willing to eat seemingly any fly you present to it, the brook trout is an enigma. I have caught dozens within minutes in remote bogs in western Maine, and have caught what I am sure is every lone trout in tiny pools in streams no more than two feet across, but I am still sometimes stumped by the brookie. I have caught only one "salter," which is a sea-run brook trout, on a nameless stream in Red Beach just below the little dam my great grandfather fell from and then died many years before. (I encountered his ghost there as I was playing that salter. Yes, I am serious. You may read the tale in *The Complete Guide to Fly Fishing Maine;* Down East Books.) There is also a salter population that comes up Maine's once nearly fatally poisoned Androscoggin River; the now productive river was nearly killed by paper mills, then brought back from the brink when furious Mainers learned the truth behind the malodious stench wafting up from the river.

The brook trout dines on all manner of aquatic and terrestrial insects, as well as smelt, dace, chubs, shiners, assorted minnows, and tiny mollusks. On Labrador's western slope giant brook trout feed on rodents like mice, shrews, and voles that fall into streams.

Brookies have been successfully transplanted far from their original range, which is from northern Georgia (the farther south one goes and the warmer the water gets, the smaller the average size of the brook trout) to

Maine, Ontario, Quebec, and the Maritimes. (Last weekend I was fishing for brookies on Colorado's Beaver Creek, while no doubt other fly-fishers were casting to them from Washington to Minnesota, South Carolina to Michigan, Idaho to Argentina and Chile.)

With its beauty, narrow environmental niche, and frequent eagerness to eat the fly you offer it, it is no wonder the brook trout is beloved.

In days gone by, Rangeley Lake (all the Rangeley Lakes, in fact), located beside the town of Rangeley, Maine, where I used to teach at the Navy Survival School (I am a retired Marine), was famous for its incredible brook trout fishing, with average fish weighing several pounds and much heavier fish being quite commonplace. Rangeley became the center for big brookies, and fishing pressure in the late 1880s was considerable. Then, in a move that still confounds many, landlocked salmon were introduced to the Rangeley Lakes and competed heavily for the available forage. The fish-

ing for both species quickly began to wane, and smelt were introduced to help feed the inhabitants. The salmon gorged themselves on the smelt (and no doubt small brookies) and the brookies ate what they could, but it was the end of the great brook trout angling in Rangeley Lake. The landlock soon surpassed the colorful char as the primary predator and is believed to be the reason behind the extirpation of blueback trout from the lake.

Today, every now and then, someone takes a big brookie from the lake, big being a few pounds, but the old days are gone and will never return. The trout are there, as they are in many other Maine

The author on Maine's remote Redington Pond.

lakes, ponds, streams, and brooks, and they are available in many states, but to get consistent trophy brook trout one must travel to Labrador, Chile, Argentina, Quebec, or certain waters in Ontario. And it is to Quebec we go to hear from Joe Stefanski, who runs a premier brook trout service on the shores of Lake Diana at Lake Diana Lodge, by Kuujjuaq, and Lake Ternay Lodge, northwest of Wabush.

SEASONS AND SIZES

Naturally you are going to have to check the regulations if you are traveling to a region unfamiliar to you, unless you will be staying at a camp or will be with a guide who will know all these things and keep you straight. Sometimes, given the northernmost climes brookies are found in, the season can be quite short; Lake Diana Lodge runs only from July to early September because it is so far north (just south of Ungava Bay).

Sizes vary radically, from 6-inch squirts like those so common in Maine's Quiggle Brook to mind-numbing mammoth trout in Labrador's Minipi River and Minonipi Lake. The heaviest brook trout ever taken on a fly was caught in Quebec's Assinica Broadback River (it weighed 10 pounds, 7 ounces). At Lake Diana the brookies average 2 pounds but run up to 6 pounds.

TACKLE

Talk about a spread. Brook trout rods start at a 7 1/2–foot, full-flex, 1-weight for skittish little guys on Redington Stream, and go to an 8 1/2– to 10-foot, mid- to tip-flex, 8-weight for husky-biting eye-poppers on the Kaniapiskau River. These are one of the few game fish that can make such a claim. Call ahead!

For small brookies you need not have a $500 reel since you can strip them in, but for trout about 2 pounds and up you will want a reel with a reasonable drag, and for 5- and 6-pound trout you should have a little better than average drag.

Lines might mean weight-forward floaters to sink-tips and full-sinks. Again, do some research and be ready.

Leaders and tippets are equally wide-ranging. For sink-tips and full-sinks you can often shorten them up quite a ways, but they should usually be longer when using a floating line, and much longer (12 feet or so) if the trout are leader shy. Leader-shy trout are not a problem at Lake Diana, but you need 8- to 10-pound test to effectively handle these biggest of brookies, which you want to play as rapidly as possible in order to release them safely. Most brookies in the states, however, can be taken with a 9-foot 5X, which tests to just under 2 1/2 pounds. You can often go lighter, too, and I fish a 6X or 7X if the pound-or-so trout are taking very small flies.

In many waters brookies have a diverse diet that often varies with the season and what is happening in and on the water. If you are fishing beaver

*Simple dry flies are often an excellent choice for
the still waters of a beaver pond.*

The Royal Coachman is often a good choice.

ponds, which frequently suffer from overpopulation, a Mosquito may be a good first choice. If the Mosquito doesn't work, perhaps a fly that imitates nothing, such as the Royal Coachman, is the answer, or even a mayfly imitation like a Light Cahill, Light Hendrickson, or A.K. Best's PMD Quill.

When brookies are feeding in streams beside fields, especially when the wind is up, you will see some explosive takes that could indicate they are feeding on terrestrials such as grasshoppers. Gentler takes may be telling you that tiny insects are being blown in instead.

In regions with a winter brook trout fishery, nymphs are the most productive. Oftentimes a caddis imitation is the way to go.

Up on Lake Diana and Lake Ternay, big flies are standard. Muddler variations, Diana Dolls, Mickey Finns, and Woolly Buggers are the streamers you will need. Dries include the Rat-faced McDougal, Bivisible, and Royal Wulff. Bombers and Buck Bugs are also good.

TACTICS

Being a char, the brookie is a bit more diverse in its diet than true trout like the brown. Whereas it is true that the brown does eat a wide array of

Winter brookies look for lies that afford them maximum protection while bringing food to them.

prey, the brookie takes it one step further by tending to eat things the brown would likely pass up. Brookies are known for their love of the strange and unusual, and flies that would scare a brown half out of the water are frequently of great interest to brook trout. The moral? Never be afraid to tie on a fly that imitates nothing or is gaudy, even disgusting, to the human eye. The brook trout might find it delightfully tempting, appealingly delectable, and completely edible.

Like browns and rainbows, brook trout can be very sensitive to your approach. I have spooked many a brookie by carelessly stomping up to the side of the brook, only to find that the trout was hiding right under the bank and took off for points north upon feeling my footfalls or seeing my shadow or silhouette.

Brookies inhabit the narrowest of streams and brooks, so the fly-fisher should never pass up a water because it looks small and confined. One of the most prolific streams I fish is quite narrow (a "two-hopper"), but it holds countless brookies ranging from 4 inches to the occasional trophy 10-incher.

I once found brookies in a nameless brook less than 2 feet wide below Maine's Black Nubble. I tipped over a nearby log and pulled a tan slug about half an inch long from beneath it. I tossed it into a tiny pool and was

Caddisfly nymphs in their cases from Maine's Cold Stream. There are more than 800 species of caddisflies in North America.

instantly rewarded with the sight of a brook trout dashing out to fetch it. The next day I returned with a primitive fly tied to imitate a slug and promptly caught the little guy. I released the 5-inch trout and know its progeny are still dining out in that miniscule brook today.

That brook runs through a forest of oak, beech, fir, spruce, mountain ash, and maple, and it is decorated with small granite rocks and a cape of rich, emerald green moss. The bottom is made of sticks, branches, and small rocks and gravel. It is quite different from Colorado's Beaver Creek, which has its headwaters between Sheep Mountain and the Williams Fork Mountains in the Arapaho National Forest. Beaver Creek is lined with willow and sage, and has a frequently hard mud and clay bottom with, as you might have guessed, lots of beaver activity. (It also gets stepped in frequently by elk, whereas that nameless Maine brook gets stepped in a lot by moose; the trout don't seem to mind.) But despite these differences, brookies are found in both.

Beavers are the brook trout's best friend. They create wonderful habitat for the trout and afford the fly-fisher some welcoming open-casting situations, but you must approach quietly (and use caution when negotiating dams, which tend to be booby-trapped with clever hidden holes that the engineers in-

Maine's South Branch of the Dead River provides small brookies in tight quarters, so something akin to a Sage 279 LL or an Orvis Ultra Fine is needed. These 2-weight, 7-foot, 9-inch rods are perfect for such a situation.

tentionally create to catch your foot and leg). Before casting—and this is sound advice for any trout situation—observe the water in the beaver pond. Are fish rising? Is there a hatch? Do you see chubs in the water? There is no need to rush up to the water and start casting; the trout aren't going anywhere and you will have a better go of it if you just relax and see what's going on before casting blindly.

Speaking of chubs, the bigger brookies will be feeding on them, so it may behoove you to use a weighted Muddler to imitate a chub, or to go with a streamer like a brown Woolly Bugger or Matuka. Once, while fishing in a beaver flowage near Maine's Keene Lake, I found what were probably thousands of chubs. They would eat my worm as soon as it hit the water, never allowing the gorgeous brookies to have a chance. Putting my 10-year-old mind to work, I ran back down Shattuck Road to my grandmother's house on Route 1 in Red Beach, and grabbed my fly rod and a Muddler Minnow from my dad's fly box. Back at the flowage, I cast the Muddler out and was promptly rewarded with a foot-long brookie, fat and marvelous.

Brook trout also live quite well in wider, slower streams. Although it doesn't look like your classic brookie water, Maine's Oyster River in West Rockport (toward Warren and below Mill Street) produces some decent fish. And even intermittent (seasonal) waters produce brookies, sometimes

Photo courtesy of the National Fresh Water Fishing Hall of Fame

Ontario's Hogan Lake gave this fine brook trout up to Larry Wilson.

in amazing numbers. One such tiny farm pond I fished as a teenager on a point overlooking the Medomak River on property owned by the Cooney family. It had a small brook running into and out of it, and in the dead of summer it would be nearly dry, but in early summer the pond was filled with trout, some as big as 10 inches.

Don't underestimate the size some brookies can reach, even in small streams. Although I haven't fished there since 1968, I used to take 14-inch brookies from the beaver ponds below Flowed Land Ponds in Red Beach, Maine, and I took some fine trout from the little pond by the Cook's house across from Red Beach Cove.

In short, the brookies might be anywhere.

Now for some arctic char and Dolly Varden.

Arctic Char and Dolly Varden

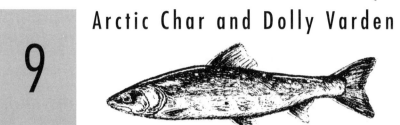

9

Chuck Ash
Brightwater Alaska Guide Service
Anchorage, Alaska

RELATIVES OF THE BROOK TROUT, ARCTIC CHAR, AND DOLLY VARDEN HAVE ALL THE attributes of fine game fish, including beauty reserved only for very special fish. Although you can catch them in the Lower 48, the best fly-fishing for them is in Alaska, as Chuck Ash can attest.

SEASONS AND SIZES

Arctic char are the bigger of the two species, growing to more than 32 pounds as compared to a little more than 18 pounds for the Dolly Varden. Dollies average between 1 and 3 pounds in the Bristol Bay watershed and some surrounding rivers and lakes, while the char grow a little bigger.

Dollies that are not landlocked (both the Dolly Varden and the char have anadromous populations as well as landlocked populations) begin to show up shortly after the salmon arrive in late June to mid-July. But the arctic char is in a bit of a different situation, according to Chuck.

"Arctic char are limited to lakes on Kodiak Island, the Bristol Bay–Alaska Peninsula region and the Arctic north of the Brooks Range. Generally, these fish are difficult to catch on a fly rod because they tend to be dispersed and are often found in fairly deep water." However, situations do exist to catch these char, as Chuck explains.

"The first situation occurs in May or June when the smolt of sockeye salmon migrate out of their nursery lake and head toward the ocean. The outlets of these lakes act as funnels, concentrating the migrating smolt. Arctic char, Dolly Varden, rainbow trout, and lake trout will all gather at these spots to take advantage of the abundant food. It is often easy to spot the schools of smolt by the activity of the gulls and terns feeding on them, or by the surface disturbance caused by predator fish attacking the smolt."

When the wind is absolutely calm, Chuck also recommends watching for char feeding on the surface of lakes like the Tikchik Lakes. Char in the

3-pound-plus range can be had under some wonderful conditions. Also, when the sockeyes come up to spawn right below the lake outlets, in the lakes themselves near the shore, in connecting rivers, and in tributary streams, char can be found feeding on the eggs.

TACKLE

Rods can start at a tip- or mid-flex 5-weight about 9 feet long, and go up to a 7-weight or thereabouts. Delicate presentations are not mandatory but accuracy can be.

The reel needs a pretty good drag system because one never knows when a large Dolly or char will suddenly replace the 2-pound fish, and with char going to 32 pounds and Dollies going to 18, you have to be ready. Better to be safe than sorry in this situation, so use a good reel.

Use floating or sink-tip lines, and sometimes mini sink-tips, Chuck advises. Leaders for streamers should be short, between 4 and 6 feet. If you use factory-made tapered leaders, buy one that is 6 or 7 1/2 feet long and trim the butt down to length. Fast-water leaders should be about 12-pound test, otherwise 8- to 10-pound is fine.

The Orvis Power Matrix rod has excellent action for arctic char and Dolly Varden on Alaska streams and rivers.

The beauty of the fish often matches that of the land.

"Fishing with nymphs and eggs requires more variation in the selection of leaders," Chuck says. "Length should be determined by the type of line used, the depth of the water, and the speed of the current. The leader may be 6 to 12 feet long when using a floating line. If water depth and conditions prevent your fly from reaching the bottom on a floating line, then switch to a sink-tip. In the interest of keeping drag to a minimum, the shorter the sink-tip section you can get away with, the better. When using a sink-tip line, a leader length of 4 to 7 1/2 feet should be right, depending on conditions.

"Dry fly-fishing for Dollies requires no more than a 7 1/2-foot leader, though there is nothing wrong with using a 9-foot leader," says Chuck.

Flies truly run the gamut for char and Dollies, and the fly you select will be very dependent on the conditions and season. Chuck recommends olive, brown, black, or purple bait fish patterns in general. Specifics include Woolhead Sculpins, Zonkers, Clouser Minnows, Thunder Creek patterns, Egg Sucking Leeches, Woolly Buggers, Red Rockets, and the Mickey Finn. The Iliamna Pinkie and Glo-Bugs are good egg patterns, but have available a selection of colors, like pale yellow-orange, champagne, dark orange, orange, and pink. When water levels fall and salmon start rotting on the shore, maggot patterns can be very productive, as can rotting-flesh patterns like a #6 Ginger Bunny. Other good decaying-flesh patterns are a #6 White Bunny, Battle Creek Special, and Woolly Buggers in white and pink.

Chuck also fishes nymphs, especially when other patterns aren't working or are working so well that he wants to try something else. Gold-ribbed Hare's Ears, #12–#14, (dark brown is good, as are bead-heads) and Flash-back Nymphs are good.

"Dry flies, like nymphs, are rarely used," says Chuck, "but they can make for some memorable days."

When the Dollies are thrashing out their redds (nests in the streambed thrashed out by spawning salmonids), Chuck will use a Royal Wulff, Adams, Elk-Hair Caddis, or Humpy. A #10 can produce nicely under the right conditions, and Chuck has seen friends catch plenty in the 5-pound range.

TACTICS

"Streamers are commonly fished on a sink-tip with a short leader, often of straight, untapered monofilament. Presentations vary, but the most successful method is to cast quartering upstream, then pause to allow the fly to sink. Once you figure that the fly is at or near the bottom, begin a series of strips punctuated by a short pause until the fly is quartered below you. At this point the current will begin to swing the fly directly downstream from you. Allow that to happen without stripping the fly. Once the fly is directly below you, let it hang in the current. After 30 seconds or so start to strip until you have retrieved enough line to allow you to cast and repeat the routine again. During this whole procedure the rod tip should be just off the surface of the water and pointed directly at your fly," Chuck says.

"Once the salmon begin to spawn, I switch my pattern of choice from a streamer to an egg imitation."

Besides using patterns that imitate decaying salmon flesh as the spawn ends and egg imitations during the spawn, Chuck goes with those maggot imitations when the salmon carcasses are exposed to the air.

"If the water subsequently rises to cover the carcasses it washes the larval flies into the current where they become available to the char. I was fishing a tributary creek out of Dillingham in late August and was having a slow day on Iliamna Pinkies in spite of an abundance of spawning sockeyes and cruising Dollies. I landed one Dolly that obviously had gorged itself. As I was unhooking it, the fish regurgitated several maggots. I switched patterns immediately and the rest of the afternoon lived up to the promise that the river had only been teasing me with up to that point.

"Anadromous Dolly Varden spend a large portion of their lives in the ocean. During most of their marine existence they are found near the shoreline and off the mouths of creeks and rivers. Ocean fishing for Dollies is best done along gravel beaches, around kelp beds, and where creeks and

Inclement weather doesn't slow the action down.

rivers enter the sea. The proper rig for fishing in these areas is a sink-tip and leader set-up similar to that used for streamer fishing in rivers. Their food consists of invertebrates, especially amphipods, and three types of bait fish: sand lances, capelins, and salmon smolt, especially those of pink salmon. The scuds that are found in fresh water are a type of amphipod and their saltwater relatives look very familiar. Ocean amphipods are 1/2 to 3/4 of an inch long and are usually gray or olive in color. Tie your scud patterns accordingly. The most effective saltwater Dolly Varden patterns, however, are those imitating sand lances and capelins. Sand lances are also known as sand eels, and there are patterns for them in most saltwater tying books. Capelins, members of the smelt family, are also known as candlefish and grunion. They are silvery in color with a narrow, elongated body. Any pattern that imitates sand lances will be close enough for capelin."

Well, Chuck Ash's knowledge of arctic char and Dolly Varden is obviously exceptional. Speaking of exceptional, let's try some bluegills now.

10

Bluegill

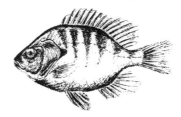

Dr. Jay
Dr. Jay's Guide Service
Raleigh, North Carolina

THE BLUEGILL IS MUCH MORE THAN THE OFT PREFERRED GAME FISH OF OUR childhood, and although Dr. Jay calls them the "Rodney Dangerfields of fish as far as many fly-fishermen are concerned," because "they get no respect," I suspect that more fly-fishers are closet bluegill lovers than we really know. I was never in that closet, I am pleased to say. Even far more clever and insightful fly-fishers than myself have acknowledged that they, too, love the bluegill, and this group includes respected fly-fishers like Nick Lyons. Bluegills are, as Nick says, generous.

Living from coast to coast—although their original range was the eastern half of the country—and inhabiting lakes, ponds, canals, drainage ditches, mosquito-control ditches, streams, and creeks, the venerable bluegill offers fine sport on very light fly-fishing tackle for anyone who doesn't mind them being anxious to strike a foam rubber spider or small popper. For their size they put up a good fight, and bluegills can be strikingly beautiful.

SEASONS AND SIZES

Bluegills run from a few ounces to—believe it or not—more than 4 pounds, but such a behemoth is exceedingly rare. The largest ever taken on a fly weighed 2 pounds, 12 ounces, and was caught in North Carolina. Most record fish come from the Southeast, although big bluegills are to be found in every state they inhabit. But in any state, a 1-pound bluegill is a worthy opponent and something to brag about.

Bluegills can be caught throughout the year, but spring and summer seem to be the best times of year, especially the late spring when the bluegills spawn and get the urge to feed heavily after the cold winter months.

TACKLE

Dr. Jay, who has a master of science and a doctorate in marine biology, recommends an 8- to 9-foot, 5- or 6-weight rod. I often use a Sage 5-weight that is 8 feet, 3 inches, but lately I have been going to a 7 1/2–foot 3-weight, and I am seriously considering a 2-weight. As a matter of fact, as soon as this book sells its first million copies, I shall call Randy Swisher at Sage and buy from him a 279 LL, which is a 2-weight, 7-foot, 9-inch rod. Yes, I shall do just that.

There is never any reason to go heavier than a 6-weight, and most casting situations call for a maximum length of 9 feet, with 7 1/2 to 8 1/2 feet being more likely.

The reel can be any balanced reel you wish. If you want to drop a few hundred bucks on a world-class reel, go right ahead, but there is no need to do so. For bluegills the reel is just a place to store the fly line, and nothing more.

Tiny poppers will often bring good results, as one did with this Minnesota bluegill.

You will use a weight-forward or double-taper floating line most frequently, but you should also have a sink-tip. You'll learn why in the tactics section.

Leaders, according to Dr. Jay, "should be 7 1/2 to 9 feet in length. Longer leaders can be used but they are often difficult to cast and are often not necessary to entice a strike. A small, 1- to 2-foot tippet (3X) can be tied to the leader to prevent the more expensive tapered leader from being shortened each time you change your fly. You may want to tie dropper loops on your leader so that two or more flies can be fished at once."

Dr. Jay recommends some flies that many bluegill lovers don't consider.

"Because of the diversity of the bluegill's diet, a number of flies can be chosen. The optimum fly will often depend on the local hatch and spawning conditions, but can include such flies as the Woolly Worm, Royal

Britta Newman and Maggie Roiger were bluegill pros before they entered the 3rd grade. Soon they will be fly-fishing for them.

Coachman, crayfish, nymphs, Muddler Minnow, Woolly Bugger, McGinty, Dave's Cricket, Mosquito, Light Cahill, Joe's Hopper, Yellowjacket, Black Gnat, ants, and assorted poppers. In other words, just about any small to moderately sized fly can nab a bluegill given the right conditions. And believe me, after a morning of 'nonfishing,' you will more than welcome the bite of these feisty creatures."

TACTICS

Whereas it is easy—well, most of the time—to catch small bluegills on a fly, the bigger bulls and fat females can be another thing altogether. And sometimes that thing can be just patience and experimentation—and patience. For instance, a friend of mine has a fantastic farm pond in North Carolina filled with giant bluegills (and some mighty impressive largemouths). I have fished it many times and usually find that I just can't walk up to the pond and start catching bluegills the size of a dinner plate. No. Usually I have to spend at least half an hour casting to half-interested fish, but then they seem to shrug and allow me to catch them, and they are big and plump and a very dark indigo blue. I have no idea why they wait for 30 minutes or so before hitting, but they do this no matter what time of the day I arrive and regardless of the conditions.

"Locating bluegills is not difficult," Dr. Jay admits. "Several factors should be considered when finding them. During spawning time, look for spawning beds in shallow, sandy or gravelly water. The spawning nests appear as doughnut-shaped depressions, usually 1 to 2 feet in diameter. Your chances of locating heavy concentrations of fish are best early in the spawning season. The fish concentrate in shallow areas where anglers can easily find them. Nest-guarding males attack flies that come too close, and females feed through the spawning period. During the early summer, bluegills thrive on mayfly nymphs. Also, they can be observed feasting on the emerging insects as they hatch out and come to the surface. Some of your hottest dry fly-fishing can be enjoyed during these periods when insects are hatching. Try to 'match the hatch' with some of the flies mentioned earlier.

"You can prolong your fishing by relocating to new waters as the season progresses," Dr. Jay adds.

"Bluegills nest earliest in shallow, murky lakes because they warm the fastest. When they complete spawning in these waters, others are just beginning their spawn cycle in deep, clear lakes. Bluegills spawn earlier in the South than in the North, with North Carolina bluegills spawning in March and April compared to May and June up north.

The right cover is always important.

"After spawning is complete and during the heat of midsummer, the fish migrate to deeper water during the day and come back into the shallows only during periods of early morning, late evening, and night. The hotter the weather and water, the later the bluegills appear to feed at night. Thus, during hot days, fish only in deep-water beds, deep drop-offs, and along steep banks and shady cool spots affording cover. In the very early morning hours, late evening, and at night, you can fish the weedy shallows where the bluegills come in to feed.

"In early fall when the temperature has cooled to about 70 degrees, bluegills will often be found all over the lake, sometimes shallow and other times deep. When the water is below 70 degrees, the shallow water is generally good when it is being warmed by a hot sun; if the weather is cold and the water is getting below ideal temperatures, bluegills will tend to migrate into deeper and deeper water. After the cold weather of fall really takes effect, most large bluegills are holding in about 10 to 15 feet of water.

"Generally, bluegills will bite better on wet flies than on dry. If the fish are not striking on the surface, sink your flies down as deeply as needed to catch the large fish. One of the most important of considerations in fly-fishing for bluegills is to fish the fly slowly. This holds for both wet and dry flies. Cast the dry fly or popper and let it rest for about 30 seconds or so

With patience and experimentation, you will catch one of these.

before twitching it. Do not drag it across the water; fish it very slowly, just barely making it flutter and then pausing quite a while between twitches.

"When fishing wet flies, let them sink for several seconds or even a couple of minutes to reach the desired depths. The proper depth can be attained using an appropriate sinking line and leader. Bluegills can be curious and will often examine a fly for some time before striking.

"Try to set the hook the instant a strike is felt or seen. Bluegills are masters at sucking in flies and then instantly spitting them out before you know what happened. Watch your line carefully and if you see or feel even the slightest touch, quickly set the hook.

"When hooked, bluegills instinctively turn their bodies at right angles to the pressure. Water resistance against the fish's broad side makes it difficult to gain line. This trait makes bluegills one of the toughest fighting panfish."

Dr. Jay has been at this for quite a spell now, as you can tell.

OK, let's get after those stripers.

part

3

ANADROMOUS GAME FISH

Striped Bass

Captain Doug Jowett
Brunswick, Maine

Captain Pat Keliher
Freeport, Maine

Captain Brian Horsley
Flat Out Guide Service
Kitty Hawk, North Carolina

We are truly fortunate to have striped bass fishing once again on the East Coast of the United States, and the fishing is phenomenal at that. But it hasn't always been this way.

The 1980s saw a severely depleted striped bass fishery from the Southeast to the Northeast due to terrible habitat loss and degradation in traditional spawning grounds and rearing areas all along the eastern seaboard, and insane overfishing by commercial and recreational anglers alike. These factors, coupled with what some fisheries biologists believe was a simultaneous cyclical decline in the population of stripers, produced one of the most dramatic and shocking falls in a game fish's population ever witnessed. Something had to be done, and it was.

Captain Doug Jowett catches another one.

A recovery program at the national level involved a massive effort by the National Marine Fisheries Service (a rare success for this often inept agency), many state fisheries departments, and recreational anglers who had seen the light. Recreational anglers self-imposed extreme restrictions on keeping stripers. As expected, the commercial fishermen fought conservation efforts tooth and nail, wanting desperately to continue their historical policies of fishing out entire stocks of fish and then moving on to the next species. Nevertheless, water quality and habitat restoration and enhancement programs were put in place and rigorously enforced. The result was the complete renewal of the Atlantic striped bass.

Today, states from Georgia to Maine enjoy a fabulous fishery for stripers (or "rockfish," as they are called in the South) that is a clear and ever-present indicator of the power of recreational anglers when they join with others of a like mind to right a wrong and do the ethical thing. And a good thing, too—the striped bass is the consummate fly tackle game fish. It grows big, fights hard, is often a sucker for the fly, and is now back in great numbers.

SEASONS AND SIZES

You guessed it. The size of the stripers you get into depends on the time of year, the watershed, skill, knowledge of where the bigger stripers reside, and luck. For instance, when Captain Doug Jowett hits the rips and surf in the Kennebec River watershed in mid-May, he knows that the first stripers of the year to show up there are "schoolies" ranging from 18 to 24 inches and weighing 3 to 6 pounds. But Doug also knows that soon after these smaller fish arrive, the bigger guys make their appearance; they will average nearly a foot longer, with the occasional 40-inch striper hitting. Fish weighing 40 pounds and then some are occasionally caught, especially right off Popham Beach and the many islands and shoals that comprise the rocky Maine coast where I spent so much of my youth.

Other Maine rivers offer good striper action, including the Sheepscot, Damariscotta, and St. George. On the St. George, which has its mouth at Port Clyde, try the "narrows" below the Maine State Prison and State Police Range in Thomaston, and the stretch above there that runs all the way up into Warren. Another good place is where the river runs below the bridge at Route 1 near the confluence with the Oyster River. There I saw an angler catch a coho salmon below what used to be the "green bridge" (now replaced by a modern structure) over Route 1 back in 1970 or 1971. He wasn't sure what he had, and when I got a look at it in his boat, I said that, although they weren't supposed to be in this river (or anywhere near it), it looked like a coho, which is what it was later identified as being.

Maine's rivers are full of surprises, and sometimes they give up weird catches like the Atlantic salmon caught at the confluence of the St. George River and Seven Tree Pond in Union in April of 1997. No one has a clue what that Atlantic salmon was doing there, but there it was. (That spot, by the way, is excellent for big browns in April and May.)

The stripers in North Carolina's Roanoke River offer some of the fastest action in the world, with fish running from a few pounds to 10 or more during the spring and early summer run. (Catches of 100 stripers a day during this time is not at all uncommon.) And San Francisco Bay offers good stripers during spring, summer, and fall in locations surprisingly close to mankind.

TACKLE

The striper is a strong fish known for its stamina. Consider that these fish run from a few pounds to 40 or so, as well as the size flies you need, and start with rods at 8-weights and go to 10-weights. (Capt. Pat Keliher prefers nothing heavier than a 10-weight.) Nine- to 10-foot rods are the norm, tip-flex or mid-flex, the latter being for schoolies.

The author works a piece of North Carolina's Atlantic Intracoastal Waterway near the mouth of the New River.

A reel resistant to saltwater, with an excellent drag capable of handling powerful runs, is a must. It must be able to hold at least 150 yards of 30-pound Dacron backing, according to Doug Jowett. If you try to stop a "green" 30-pound striper using a reel with a questionable drag, the striper is likely to win without a contest.

Lines range from weight-forward or shooting head floating, to full-sink 300- to 450-grain lines, and include sink-tips and intermediates if you are fishing anywhere in the Northeast, but in North Carolina's Roanoke you will be using mostly floating and intermediate lines. The conditions in the Northeast (Rhode Island to Maine) are more diverse than those in North Carolina or elsewhere in the South. One minute you could be casting big pencil poppers off Carrying Place Head and the next you might be fishing a deep rip in the Jaquish Gut (the latter of which, by the way, is stupendous for tinker mackerel in June).

"Leaders do not need to be complicated," says Doug. "I use a 40-pound, 10-inch butt leader with a double surgeon's loop for quick changes of leaders. To that I add a 3-foot section of 15- to 20-pound mono followed by a 2-foot, 20- to 40-pound shock tippet. Every section is connected using a loop-to-loop system. The lighter mid-section of the system allows breaking off the tip when caught on the bottom while currents and close proximity to ledges require a quick retreat. It's a lot less expensive to leave a fly on the rocks where expensive boat or motor damage can happen quickly."

Pat adds that some situations require a line with a saltwater taper or a super fast-sinking line. A saltwater taper design can vary by manufacturer. Some shorten the head starting at about 10-weight, others don't. Experiment to see what works best for you. Larger flies with heavy lines are easier to pick up and cast with a saltwater taper, reducing false casts, which can be important when targeting stripers and other saltwater game fish that can appear and disappear in no time flat.

The coating on some lines is better for abrasion resistance, which is important because rocks and lobster pot lines are commonplace. Check the manufacturer's description of the lines.

The flies to use are pretty simple. Deceivers and Clousers in sizes 1 through 4/0, but have some 6/0s on hand just in case. Doug's "bread and butter" is "a 4 1/2–inch, 3/0 streamer, white in color with a topping of chartreuse and peacock herl with a 1/36-ounce, nickel-plated lead eye and pearl Flashabou siding on the wing."

He adds that, "When the menhaden are in, we use a super large bunker in numerous colors but mostly white with a lot of flash in sizes 4/0 to 6/0. These honkers can be up to 10 inches long. Then there are days when a simple cork or foam popper in size 1/0 will do the trick."

TACTICS

Your tactics will be dictated by the region and season. For example, I focus on bridge abutments, dock pilings, and sea walls when I fish North Carolina's Neuse River—which, frankly, I don't do often because agricultural runoff has caused massive algae growths and pfiesteria, a flesh-eating microbe that has killed many of the river's fish. But when I am fishing in Maine, everything changes. I may be casting into the surf of Popham Beach with a striping basket around my waist, working a rip beside Wooden Ball, or hitting a seam off Matinicus Island, where I fished for cod and pollock as a boy under the tutelage of Maine's most respected charter captain (now retired), Bill Gargan, a living legend who still makes his home on Spruce Head Island.

"There are five basic elements to locations where stripers are found," says Doug. "They are: current, feed, structure, structure, and structure.

"The habitat where stripers are found is consistently intimidating to most people. If the areas you are fishing most of the time aren't a little scary, you aren't fishing in the right place. Heavy current and ledge structure are the keys to consistent success with stripers on a day-to-day basis, especially for the big fish.

"I have one honey-hole that is 50 feet or less long. At certain times on the going tide it will always produce

An angler weighs a Neuse River striper, one of an ever-decreasing population suffering from pollution.

fish. It's a tough spot. The current is strong, there is an eddy that will put you into a sharp ledge, and you only have time for two or three casts during the drift through and you must use a super fast-sinking tip on a fairly long cast. Add wind and swells to the formula, and you begin to understand the precise nature of learning to read your water.

"The rougher the situation is, the more likely you will connect with fish. There's only one way to learn and that's to study coastal charts closely and get out there as often as possible to figure out each potential hot spot.

"Large ledges and points are obvious places to concentrate on. As you learn to read a chart and experience tidal flows on the water, you will learn to read some great fishing locations. Look for some type of small structure where low-tide water levels are 0–10 feet but close to 30–60 feet of water. That structure will produce some big rip currents when the tide flows by, especially during the ebb tide.

"On the off season, go out and float a complete tide cycle several times to observe where these rips develop during different stages of the tide. The time spent floating tides will provide you with a lifetime of knowledge to work with. Keep a log book. There are thousands of potentials you can't keep track of in your head. It takes years on the water to be consistent in hooking stripers under the many variables thrown at you daily.

"I have one section of water I'm studying. I'm on the water more than 100 days a season and figure this new area will take me four to five years to learn intimately. Successful striped bass fishing is no accident. Study, study, study, and think current, feed, structure, structure, and structure. Success will be yours."

Night can be an exciting striper situation, as Capt. Brian Horsley knows. He fishes in all sorts of weather and doesn't mind getting wet if there's a striper in it for him. The inlets and surf are his realm, and there are often great runs of stripers available right from the beach and rocks. Anyone would be crazy to pass up the opportunity for some big stripers such as those found on the Outer Banks.

Steelhead are coming up.

Steelhead

Bob Pigott
Port Angeles, Washington

THE STEELHEAD IS AN ALMOST LEGENDARY GAME FISH, KNOWN FOR ITS BONE-jarring runs and phenomenal ability to melt a fly reel in short order. They are available to fly-fishers from the Northeast (especially New York State), across to the Great Lakes region (Michigan and Minnesota have excellent runs), all the way to the other side of the country in evergreen-studded Washington. Actually a true Pacific salmon, the steelhead is the type of deranged game fish that commands a legion of admirers to face the rigors of severe weather and icy streams—all for the chance to feel the rod-creaking power of the mighty fish.

Washington's famed Olympic Peninsula is one of North America's top steelhead destinations, and on that peninsula dwells one Bob Pigott, known far and wide as the man to

Bob Pigott maneuvers his drift boat down the Sol Duc River.

listen to when it comes to steelhead in that neck of the woods. But he had better watch his back, because his daughter is currently training to become a fly-fishing guide specializing in taking women fly-fishing out that way.

SEASONS AND SIZES

The Olympic Peninsula does offer genuine steelhead action throughout the year, including bracing days in the dead of winter. But spring, summer, and fall are best, with spring and summer being top notch. As is the case with so many other species, steelhead across North America can be caught to varying degrees depending on where and when you are fishing and what the local conditions are, so, as always, do your homework before going somewhere unfamiliar.

Steelhead are large, powerful fish that can easily weigh 20 pounds or more. They are known for their strong runs, and long fights are commonplace.

TACKLE

According to Bob, steelhead on the Olympic Peninsula require fly rods ranging from 6- to 9-weight. A steelhead on a 6-weight rod is not a fish to be trifled with, so your fighting skills absolutely have to equal or better

Bill Dawson and Bob Pigott with an Olympic Peninsula steelhead.

those of your opponent. In fast water, handling an irate steelhead on a 6-weight can be nerve wracking to say the least, since the crafty fish knows exactly how to use the weight and power of the water, along with the rocks and other structure in the watercourse, to its advantage. This leaves little room for mistakes.

A 9-weight rod is able to cast a fly better on windy days, and it can better handle a large steelhead bent on putting as much space between itself and the fly-fisher as possible, in as short a time as possible.

As far as reels are concerned, drag is the most important consideration. Steelhead are one of the most powerful species on the continent when it comes to doing battle with a fly-fisher, and they love to try to empty a reel of its line and backing, which should be at least 100 yards of 20-pound test backing. Cheap reels with drags that can't take the pressure aren't an option with steelhead.

When it comes to lines for steelhead, Bob recommends floating double tapers or sink-tip type III or IV.

"There are two separate runs of steelhead in this area: winter and summer. Winter steelhead call for flies in size 4 to 2/0, while summer steelhead demand the same type of flies but in sizes 2 to 12," says Bob. "The traditional steelhead patterns include shrimp, leech, and speys."

TACTICS

Bob fishes eight steelhead rivers on the Olympic Peninsula: the Sol Duc, Bogachield, Calawah, Hoh, Quillayute, Clearwater, Queets, and Elwha. He says the best things about fly-fishing in this region, besides the "many happy steelhead" there, are the solitude, beautiful rivers, and terrific scenery. He is so enamored with the fishery that he feels "all days are good, whether or not you catch fish." Fortunately, those fishing with him seldom go skunked.

When I first fished with Bob, I soon learned how important he felt certain lies were. We hadn't been in his drift boat more than one minute when he maneuvered us to the far bank and jammed the boat aground. He directed me to work the fly in a pulsating motion in a very specific area of the river and not to bother casting to any other location from that particular spot. He went on to say that the steelhead would move into favored lies and stay there for a while, then move on if nothing came their way.

The fly's speed was equally important with Bob. As we moved with the current Bob would slowly row backwards, maintaining the correct speed as our lines paid out in front of us. We created the pulsating action of the fly by just lifting our rod tips a foot or so and then allowing the fly to drift back again.

Photo courtesy of the National Fresh Water Fishing Hall of Fame

Wisconsin's Root River offers excellent steelhead action.

Each time we came to a confluence where some smaller stream flowed into the river, Bob would spend extra time and energy. Several times we hauled out and waded an area that Bob knew to be productive. Eagles soared overhead while diving ducks and dippers cavorted in the river. My first strike came at a confluence, but the small fish raced upstream faster than I could strip in and it was off after one spinning leap beside the boat.

The best fish of the day came when my brother-in-law Nick had his fly attacked by what was clearly a very large steelhead. It had just begun to rain; we were about 200 yards above the take-out when Nick's rod doubled over. He set the hook a split second too late and the great fish was gone, a steelhead Bob said obviously "had some shoulders."

But steelhead fishing isn't always about unseen fish. In New York, Michigan, and other states, steelhead are available for sight-casting in narrow, clear streams where seeing a dozen fish in one glance is routine.

Try steelhead for a terrific fight often in serene locations. For another type of challenge, try salmon, which deserve their fine reputation. Let's learn about them.

Salmon

13

Chuck Ash
Brightwater Alaska Guide Service
Anchorage, Alaska

Andre Godin
Miramichi Inn
Red Bank, New Brunswick

YOU'RE GOING TO LOVE THIS CHAPTER.

If there is one type of fish that anglers are more likely to spend great gobs of money to fish for, it is salmon. Not just any salmon, mind you, but legendary fish like Chinook (king), sockeye (red), chum (dog), pink (humpy), silver (coho), and the prestigious Atlantic salmon, including the landlocked salmon, the completely freshwater version of the Atlantic salmon. This chapter takes a look at all these species, with the first part of the chapter devoted to salmon fishing in Alaska (the best Pacific salmon fly-fishing on the continent), and the second part focused on the mighty Atlantic salmon (with special attention going to the quasi-mythical Miramichi River in New Brunswick). And to tell you about them we have secured the wisdom of two highly respected professionals: Chuck Ash and Andre Godin.

Yes, you are truly blessed.

Alaska Salmon

SEASONS AND SIZES

"The general timing for Alaska is that sockeyes and kings run in June and July, chums and pinks in July and August, and silvers in August and September," says veteran salmon guide Chuck Ash. "Most runs last only three weeks or so, but there are some exceptions when silvers will trickle into a particular river all fall and winter, or when the king salmon run is split into two distinctive 'early' and 'late' runs. The trick, of course, is to show up when the fish do. A week too early and you miss the bright fish or the height of the run or the whole shebang," he advises. "To confuse the issue even further, different drainages can be different with respect to timing. To stack the odds of getting it right you need to do your homework. Read everything you can about the timing of the various salmon runs in the area you intend to fish. Talk to knowledgeable friends or fly shops or guides. This gathering of accurate information is absolutely critical. If you show up with all the right gear at the wrong time, it's going to slant your outlook on life."

Well, Chuck sure has a way with metaphors. Here's some more advice.

"The first consideration should be to decide which species of salmon you want to fish for. If you are after a long, hard fight with a big fish, then king salmon are the obvious choice. Kings average 30 to 50 pounds in most drainages, and some rivers have genetic stocks that run larger. Alaska's Kenai River, for example, gives up an occasional 80- or 90-pound fish.

"If your tastes run more to spunkier fish in greater numbers, you should look to sockeye or silver salmon. Both are 4- to 12-pound fish and both are strong fighters with a decided tendency to go aerial when hooked. Silvers average slightly heavier than sockeyes, and of all the species of salmon they are the most responsive to a fly. Sockeyes, on the other hand, run in unsurpassed numbers, especially in particular regions such as the rivers that feed Bristol Bay. When the sockeyes are parading upstream in a column three fish wide, nose-to-tail, night and day, it makes little difference that they are more reluctant to bite than other salmon.

"In most drainages, pinks are only present in significant numbers every other year. This is a result of their life cycle. They are also the smallest of the salmon, averaging somewhere around 3 or 4 pounds. Some fly-fishers

The fight is on!

discount pinks as a sport fish, but if they are fished early in their run when they are bright, they are eager and feisty. The best fishing tends to be close to the ocean.

"Chum salmon are roughly the same size as silvers and they take to a fly readily enough, but they lack the showy, line-ripping runs of silvers and sockeyes. As a result, they are not a primary target species for most fly-fishers. Nevertheless, the same premise applies to chums as to pinks: If you find them bright and close to the ocean, they can fill your day."

TACKLE

"Rod and line size are critical, so this is the logical place to start your decision-making process. Much salmon fishing is done on relatively large water for big fish under windy conditions. A high-quality rod with a fast taper is essential. It has the power to throw a big fly into the wind and will give you the reserve power in the butt section to fight the combination of powerful fish in moving water. Salmon will test the limits of your gear, and the bigger the fish and the stronger the water the easier it is for things to go awry. Quality and design are both a hedge in the favor of durability. A spare rod is also a good idea, especially on an extended or remote trip.

The right rod and line are necessary when these are the goal.

"Line size should be determined by the species of salmon and the nature of the water you will be fishing. Bigger fish and bigger water require bigger line sizes. King salmon demand a 9- or 10-weight line. If in doubt, go heavier for kings. Sockeyes, chums, and silvers require a 7- or 8-weight outfit and the same rule of doubt applies. Pinks can be readily handled with a 6- or 7-weight; opt for a 7-weight on big water and a 6-weight for small or slow water.

"Because salmon cease to feed once they enter fresh water, they lack the grab-and-gulp response typical of competitively feeding fish. Instead, they tend to mouth a fly and release it. The resulting take is soft. It usually amounts to no more than a brief hesitation in your drift or, at best, a slight tug. Choose line types that minimize drag to increase sensitivity to such a subtle take. River conditions vary, however, so no single type of line will do it all. A minimum line selection should include a weight-forward, floating line and a 10-foot, weight-forward, sink-tip line with a sink rate of at least 5 inches per second. Another specialty line that many anglers find useful is a mini sink-tip with a 4- to 5-foot sink-tip section. Its niche is defined by those conditions when a floating line won't get down to the fish and a 10-footer digs too deep too quickly. A line with a high-density, 20- to 30-foot sink-tip is occasionally of value in deep, fast-moving water. These conditions are encountered most often when fishing for kings. A full-sinking line has very limited application for the majority of salmon fishing. It creates too much drag in moving water. Its forte is ocean fishing for salmon in relatively deep water."

As you can tell by now, Chuck has this down pat. About backing, he goes on to say that kings require 250 to 300 yards of 30-pound test. Sockeyes, chums, and silvers need 150 to 200 yards of 20-pound backing, but 30-pound is fine, too. For pinks go with a like amount of 20-pound backing.

Insofar as leaders and tippets, Chuck advises that your tippet be lighter than your backing, since, if the fish empties your reel, you want your tippet to break and not the backing. He also says to be sure and have a thick enough leader butt to turn the fly over. Also, add tippet if split shot or twist-ons are adversely affecting your drift. Leaders should run 6 to 12 feet, depending on the depth. (Switch to a sink-tip line if 12 feet of leader isn't enough to get you down.) Sink-tip lines require less leader—4 to 9 feet is about right. Floating lines need more.

For reels, Chuck says a palming rim is important for adding pressure to a smooth reel with a reliable disc drag. The reel's capacity should be appropriate for the species of salmon, i.e., kings require a larger reel because of the longer runs and heavier line they demand. Spools may have to be changed quickly, so a reel that offers an easy spool change is preferable.

Chuck has found that color, contrast, flash, and action are the critical factors in determining a productive fly.

"Colors should be bright. Fuschia and fluorescent pink, lime, orange, and chartreuse all seem to be good producers, but don't discount dark colors, especially purple and black.

"Contrast also seems to be important. Work with different color combinations to achieve contrast, and include white in the possibilities.

"Flash is another critical element. The reason may be increased visibility or it may trigger an aggressive response or a latent feeding response, but for whatever reason, a little Flashabou or Krystal Flash included in the wing or tail will often make a pattern more attractive to salmon.

"Lastly, the action of the material will increase a fly's effectiveness. The best materials in this department are marabou and rabbit fur. The movement of the current will given even a resting fly apparent motion and the slightest movement of the line will cause the fly to pulsate.

"Flies for king salmon should be tied on hook sizes ranging from 1/0 to 3/0. Size 2 hooks are right for chum and silver salmon patterns, and size 6 will do nicely for pink. Weight them all.

"Sockeye salmon are somewhat of an anomaly when it comes to selecting patterns. The rules about color and contrast hold well enough and even a little bit of flash is OK, but don't make your sockeye flies big or bulky. Sockeyes prefer small, sparsely dressed flies, which are best tied unweighted or lightly weighted on a number 4 or 6 hook."

With many years of experience, Chuck Ash is able to give specific advice on what flies to have along for what waters. He says each drainage seems to have salmon with specific preferences. For the Bristol Bay area, he recommends Woolly Buggers, Egg-Sucking Leeches, Alaskabous, flash flies, and bunny flies. Kings, chums, pinks, and silvers will all fall for these patterns tied in the right size. Sockeyes go for the Gold Comet, Sockeye Orange and Sockeye Green, and the Montana Brassie.

TACTICS

Our guide has definite ideas on tactics, as you might expect. For instance, Chuck advises watching not only for jumping salmon, but for rolling or porpoising salmon, and also to keep an eye out (wearing your polarized sunglasses) for slight disturbances of the surface that indicate activity just below. The polarized sunglasses help you see individual fish in the shallows.

Forget targeting salmon moving upstream at that moment. Except for kings, salmon moving upstream will be near the bank because the current is less there, so focus instead on "holding" fish taking a breather in lies

Salmon moving steadily upstream near the bank aren't your best target.

where a break in the current occurs. These lies take shape in eddy lines at the edges of sloughs, in pocket water behind rocks and boulders, in areas of reduced current in the lee of points, bars, and islands, or in quiet water behind debris piles.

Long casts are key. Salmon spook easily and getting too close or being too noisy will spook them or make them refuse to bite.

Presentation is everything, according to Chuck, with a dead drift being the most productive most of the time. You have to have enough slack to get the fly down to where the salmon are, but you also have to have enough tension to feel the strike. Flies drifted right through pods of holding salmon get far more strikes than flies drifted above those pods.

When the dead drift fails, add a twitch and a pause. Then switch to an active retrieve if that doesn't pan out. Try an across-stream retrieve and then a direct upstream retrieve. Vary your strips and pauses in length. Sometimes long pauses are right on the money.

Successfully playing a salmon means getting him on the reel as quickly as possible. This avoids "fits and starts" and line burn. Salmon tend to panic, too, if you apply too much pressure early in the fight, which can make them run into the fast water where you will have a much longer fight.

Chuck advises playing the salmon like a trout and then releasing it safely after resuscitating it. Use barbless hooks to facilitate this.

Can you handle a salmon like this?

Well, now we know the deal on fly-fishing for Alaskan salmon. Let's head to New Brunswick and the fabulous Miramichi (where an average of 200,000 Atlantic salmon return from the ocean each year) for the most aristocratic game fish as expounded upon by Andre Godin.

Atlantic Salmon

SEASONS AND SIZES

Andre, who lives on the Miramichi River and runs the Miramichi Inn, divides the seasons into three: spring (April 15 to May 15), when "tens of thousands of salmon" are found in the river, having stayed the winter after spawning the previous fall. Andre says: "They are hungry and take the fly eagerly, with fishermen taking from 10 to 15 a day. Spring fishing is the best kept secret on Atlantic salmon." (These salmon will begin to feed heavily on their way back to the Atlantic Ocean, and the fishing can be fantastic. Fly-fishers catch up to 35 salmon a day during the spring run.)

The next season is summer, which includes June, July, and August. Andre tells us that ". . . in June, the world's largest run of salmon begins on the Miramichi. The fish are fat and sea-bright. The silvery shadows move up river, pausing, stopping, and moving again with changing water levels. Cast your fly. With helpful, professional guides, experience the rise and the sudden take of an Atlantic salmon, the landing and the release in the wild, verdant setting of this great salmon river."

Autumn salmon are fish of September and October, when the hills of New Brunswick are ablaze with the glory of the Maritime fall. Beech, maple, oak, and mountain ash all erupt in a display savored by the children of nature in halcyon days born of bracing autumn air and the spine-tingling call of a distant bull moose.

Come autumn, Andre says: "The water is full of salmon as the newly arrived fish join the summer-run residents. The river waters are cool and the salmon play in the long holding pools, providing spectacular aerial shows and slow-motion rises to the fly against a backdrop of brilliant fall foliage. The biggest fish are now in the river, waiting for the right cast and the right fly."

Sizes vary considerably. Spring salmon are smallest and run from 10 pounds or so up into the 20s. Grilse—the young salmon believed to be sexually immature—will be a little smaller. By autumn you might see salmon in the 40-pound range, perhaps bigger from time to time.

TACKLE

Rods should be 8- or 9-weights, 9 or 10 feet long. For the spring bring a sink-tip and a floating line to cover all water conditions. Your reel needs 100 yards of 30-pound test backing, and the salmon may very well get into that backing. (Rods with a quick tip and lots of backbone mean you can play the fish faster and therefore release it sooner and in better condition.)

Dry flies: #2–#4 Canuel, Haystack, Irresistible, LeFrancois, and the Rat-faced McDougal.

Bombers: #2–#4 Brown Bomber, Grizzly Hackle, Orange, and White.

Bugs: #4–#8 Green Body, Red Butt, Shady Lady, and Smurf.

Wet flies: #4–#6 (with a few #2–#8 for high and low water extremes) Big Intervale Blue, Bear, Black Ghost, Blue Charm Hairwing, Butterfly (tied with open wings and white and yellow polar bear hair; avoid getting the hair if the bear is awake, or still alive for that matter), Colburn, Copper Killer, Green Highlander, Muddler Minnow, Mitchell, Squirrel Tail, Red, Taylor Special, and the Undertaker.

Tactics for Atlantic salmon can make all the difference.

TACTICS

It has been said that fly-fishing for Atlantic salmon is a game of casting, casting, and casting again into the same lie until the salmon finally decides it has seen enough of your fly and smacks it. This might be true, but the best Atlantic salmon anglers know that presentation can make the difference between a good day and a great day.

Observe the pool where the salmon are waiting. What is the current like? In strong current try casting at an angle downstream and mend the line to reduce drag. In water running somewhere between fast and slow, cast across the current at a right angle and mend if needed. The slowest water sometimes calls for a slight upstream retrieve with the occasional pause and flutter.

Dead drifts can work, too, but experiment to see what works best. If you see other anglers catching fish using similar casts and retrieves, ask them what fly they are using. By changing from a dry to a classic salmon wet fly like the Green Highlander (just like the one I have mounted on my den wall, tied by Bruce Busby), you can suddenly crack the code.

Check typical salmon lies that aren't right in a pool. Slight changes in current speed, be they from a submerged, unseen rock, an eddy, or what have you, can mean a salmon holding there.

Perhaps more than anything, Atlantic salmon fishing means getting your fly into a lie or holding area and keeping it there as long as possible, looking like something worth biting.

Landlocked Salmon

I took my first landlocked salmon on a Gray Ghost back in the late 1960s from Maine's Alford Lake. I can't say how many landlocks I have caught since then, but the number surely isn't small. (Keep in mind, however, that many Mainers can say that the number of landlocks *they* have caught isn't exactly small, either.) Every one of these fish was caught in Maine, although upstate New York, New Hampshire, and

Photo courtesy of Maine Department of Inland Fisheries and Wildlife

A Maine Department of Inland Fish & Wildlife specialist weighs a spring landlocked salmon.

Vermont all have some good landlock fishing. Argentina, on waters like the Rio Traful, offers what I am told is the finest landlock angling available on the planet. My sources, however, also inform me that Jupiter's moon, Europa, recently discovered to have water beneath a lot of ice, may in fact have better landlock angling than even Argentina can boast about. Having been schooled by the greatest landlocked salmon angler alive, Wesley "Mel" Waters of Warren, Maine—a reference my father would have a problem with—and having fished all the great Maine landlock waters (Sebago Lake, the West Branch of the Penobscot, the Rapid River, the Kennebago, the Kennebec, and many others), I feel qualified to take this section as my own, with due regard to Mel and some other Maine anglers who know the landlock and have given me wisdom over the years.

The landlocked salmon (*Salmo salar*) is, taxonomically, an Atlantic salmon (*Salmo salar*) that, eons ago, decided not to return to the ocean; it stayed in fresh water and prospered there. It does not grow to the size of an anadromous Atlantic salmon, but it maintains every bit of spunk and

Photo courtesy of Maine Department of Inland Fisheries and Wildlife

Smelt are the landlock's most important forage fish.

its penchant for aerial antics as its traveling brother. Inhabiting lakes, ponds, rivers, and streams, it feeds heavily on smelt and other bait fish (dace, chubs), but also eats aquatic insects and terrestrials like certain moths, caterpillars, spiders, crickets, grasshoppers, and leafhoppers. What a particular landlock feeds on most depends upon the water it lives in; some feed mostly on smelt because that is the prevalent forage, and others feed more heavily on aquatic insects. Nevertheless, the rainbow smelt is crucial to the health and growth of a population of landlocks.

SEASONS AND SIZES

Landlocks are available to the fly-fisher in New England from about May to October. Mid-May to mid-June and September are most productive. Spring landlocks tend to be sleeker and are called "racers," while autumn fish are frequently much fatter and are called "footballs."

The average landlock runs less than 2 pounds, but 5- and 6-pound fish are not uncommon, and occasionally someone comes in with one much heavier, almost always from a lake. But some rivers and streams, especially in Maine, are known to produce big landlocks come fall. One such river is the Kennebago, where the Steep Bank Pool is known more than any other as a producer of giant landlocks weighing nearly 10 pounds. What the average landlock loses in size, it makes up for—with interest—in fight.

TACKLE

Consider the water, conditions, and average size of the landlocks therein. For average fish in moderate conditions, cast a 6-weight tip-flex to mid-flex with dry flies, wet flies, nymphs, and small streamers. Cast a tip-flex 8-weight in faster water with a bit of a breeze when the landlocks are bigger and the streamers a little larger.

Landlocks will make runs, but they seldom empty a reel. They are more known for their leaps (they are nicknamed *the leaper*) than long, reel-draining runs. You can get away with any mid-range Hardy, Abel, Sage, Orvis, Scientific Anglers, Lamson, or Bean reel with no worries.

Weight-forward lines are good regardless of the conditions, and, depending on the conditions, you may need a floating, sink-tip, or full-sink line. Fish holding deep in heavy current in a small pool call for a fast full-sink. Fish in 3 feet of pocket water need a floating line. Sink-tips and slow full-sinks come in handy when dead drifting Woolly Buggers in a lake when the fish are cruising between 8 and 12 feet.

Just as for any other salmon, leaders depend primarily on depth. For most situations, 8 to 10 feet is fine. 2X (4 1/2–pound test), 3X (just under 4-pound test), and 4X (just over 3-pound test) are generally all I ever need. If I am casting larger streamers, I may go to a more stout leader with a heavier butt section.

Your fly selection should include an assortment of the following:

Streamers: Black Ghost, Gray Ghost, Green Ghost, Kennebago Smelt (created by Bud Wilcox, who's still the top salmon man in Rangeley, Maine, where he showed me how to tie this fly), Nine-Three, Warden's Worry, Queen Bee, and Supervisor (all in single or tandem).

Dry flies (in all sizes): Elk Hair Caddis, Rat-faced Irresistibles, Wulffs, Henryville Specials (a George Misko favorite) Goddard Caddis, Stimulators, Green Drakes, Dark and Light Hendricksons, Blue Duns, Light Cahills, Royal Coachmen (though this fly doesn't imitate anything real), Blue Wing Olives, March Browns, and Quill Gordons.

Wet flies: Parmacheene Belles (named after the lake in Maine), Leadwing Coachmen, Hornbergs, and Woolly Worms.

Nymphs: Gold-ribbed Hare's Ears, Princes, Pheasant Tails, Brassies, Hendricksons, Zug Bugs, and Fur Caddis Pupae.

Terrestrials: Joe's Hoppers, Dave's Hoppers, Black Ants, and Black Jassids.

TACTICS

Landlocked salmon tactics depend on the season and water you are fishing. For instance, if I am fishing Maine's Rapid River (my favorite pool is Chub Pool just above Pond-in-the-River) in June, I focus very heavily on fish holding at the end of chutes, lying in wait for smelt. I fish four primary flies: the Black Ghost, Gray Ghost, Green Ghost, and Kennebago Smelt—all single-hook streamers, of course. (These four flies are the most productive spring patterns for Maine landlocks. I would feel very confident venturing onto any water in Maine with them come spring.)

If the fish are not holding at the base of a chute, I hit the pools and pay close attention to any lie that looks like it would afford a salmon a place to hide and rest while watching for smelt.

On a warmer afternoon, do not hesitate to drift a nymph (caddis and mayfly imitations) with a strike indicator. Landlocks eat far more aquatic insects than most people realize, and they will not hesitate to eat nymphs (even duns and spinners) despite a hoard of smelt in the water around them.

Summer landlocks are a different story. With the smelt thinning out (the spawning run is over by late spring), landlocks focus on whatever is available, but feed less heavily on the whole. As water temperatures climb, seek out deeper pools and fish on cloudy days with a wind, if possible. The landlocks might pick up any fly at this time, but observe small hatches and subtle takes. Don't think that terrestrials won't do any good; they just might.

Autumn landlock fishing can be very productive, although it does not often produce strike after strike like some spring fishing. Autumn landlocks are interested in spawning, and they have had all spring and summer to feast on the wealth of forage available. This means they will be very selective, although those fish hooked tend to be quite fat.

Autumn fly-fishing often requires hitting the very same lie again and again until a holding salmon decides to eat. There is some difference of opinion here. Some experts feel that, landlocks being taxonomically identical to Atlantics, they do not actually strike a fly out of hunger but out of some ingrained reflexive response to other stimuli. Others feel that the landlocks are actually feeding and cite a tremendous difference between the "striking" habits of Pacific and Atlantic salmon: that Pacific salmon don't feed during the spawn because they "know" they are going to die soon

Photo courtesy of Maine Department of Inland Fisheries and Wildlife

Streamer patterns for landlocks.

thereafter (so why eat?), whereas Atlantics do not necessarily die after spawning and therefore feel it is prudent to eat when necessary.

I haven't a clue as to the truth of the matter, and honestly, neither does anyone else. Gut instinct? I feel landlocks in the autumn spawn strike out of agitation and annoyance. Why do I think this? Because I don't think they are especially hungry.

How's that for Maine logic?

In any case, remember to hit any lie that looks good from a trout's point of view, and remember in the fall to keep hitting good-looking lies again and again. Cast a variety of flies if nothing happens with the traditional streamers.

Also try dead drifting in a variety of situations. The tactic seems to work best at the tail of a pool, but another excellent location is at the end of a chute or run.

The author with a typical Rapid River spring landlock taken on a dead-drifted Green Ghost.

Now let's arm ourselves for battle with bluefish.

part

4

SALTWATER GAME FISH

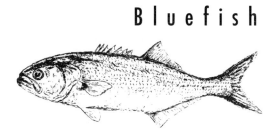

Bluefish

Captain Brian Horsley
Flat Out Guide Service
Kitty Hawk, North Carolina

Bluefish

IN THE SUMMER OF 1973, I FOUND MYSELF A BIT PERPLEXED. THE STRIPER FISHING had fallen off in the waters around Thomaston, Maine, and I was trying to find some other very big fish to get my heart racing. A vicious rumor circulating along the coast from Kittery to Machias told of giant, marauding bluefish, but this unconfirmed rumor was not being accepted at face value by many people. After all, the story was that the blues hadn't hit the Maine coast since the stock market crashed in 1929, and now we were hearing they were suddenly and mysteriously back, weighing 10–15 pounds, and tearing up bait fish like a Cuisinart thrashing a rotten mackerel.

Since it couldn't be true, John Shesler and I launched the boat at the public landing in Thomaston (in a harbor much smaller and far less busy than it is today) and motored out into the St. George River to try our luck with the supposedly toothy, ornery, and available bluefish.

Five minutes later I was nearly yanked from the boat.

The rod shuddered and the reel made a disturbingly high-pitched squeal that said my line was heading out toward Tenants Harbor and Port Clyde like never before. I clearly remember my first words to John when I realized I wasn't hung on a lobster pot: "I'll never get him in! I'll never get him in!" (John, seeing the fish leap from the water, was busy searching for his gun, but he had left it behind.) But I did get him in, and the next 12-pounder, too.

The blues had come home, Down East.

Every summer, we found ourselves again and again on the river, often catching so many big bluefish that it would take us hours to clean them beneath the umbrella tree in John's yard. His father, Dr. Lawrence Shesler (the town dentist), would come out to inspect the catch, and his wonderful and kind mother, Betty, would take a small bit of a blue and feed it to Speck, their cantankerous money cat (a breed of cat with a thick, multi-colored coat). We would divide up the fish and I, smelling to high heaven, would head back home, where the blues would feed the Newman clan—all seven of us—as well as our neighbors, the Adams, the Flecks, and the Jacksons. Life was good.

John and I continued to catch spectacular numbers of blues every summer, but fate came calling one day in the form of a strapping Marine recruiter with a jagged purple scar on his right cheek, and before I could reel in I was off to a distant spit of land infested with torturous sand fleas and steaming in the broiling heat of Dixie—Parris Island.

Many long, often exciting, and occasionally terrifying years later, I would greet John beside the trout pond in L.L. Bean's store in Freeport, Maine, where I was fortunate enough to be signing books and conducting catch-and-release demonstrations amid the chunky brook trout in the pond. John hadn't aged a day, it seemed, which is more than I can say for my weathered mug, a lined and squinty visage that tells the tale of desert combat, mysterious jungles, and jumping out of perfectly good airplanes far too many times. And as fate would have it, John, too, had become a writer, and he would soon pen a most poignant and telling foreword for my book, *The Complete Guide to Hunting in Maine*.

The only member of its family, the bluefish has cute nicknames like "chopper," "snapper," and "marine piranha," and with good reason: They have a mouth packed with some of the sharpest teeth in the ocean, and they really get a kick out of using them. That is a warning you should heed and heed well, for I have experienced the bluefish's teeth and wish for you to avoid them.

The bluefish, one of the Atlantic's most notorious infidels, is loved by many. John and I have born witness to hundreds of bloody, night-of-the-living-dead attacks upon menhaden ("pogies") in the St. George by killer bluefish that truly appeared to enjoy the mayhem and gore. I remember the first time we saw pogies jump onto the shore to save themselves from the gnashing incisors of the crazed blues, and I remember the first time a bluefish crashed into the side of my aluminum boat as it pursued a mortified pogy. I also remember the time John and I caught 17 big blues on one tide and had to leave because they had destroyed all our tackle. (The truth be known, John caught 12 of those 17.)

Bluefishing is a sport of shouts, commands, line burns, melted drags, trashed flies, and sunburns. You have to try it.

SEASONS AND SIZES

I have caught blues weighing from less than a pound to 16 pounds, from Florida to Maine. At the moment, however, the western Atlantic bluefish populations are something like 84 percent less than what they were in the mid-70s. Some anglers new to the sport who go out nowadays and catch two or three 7-pound blues scoff at the tales we tell of days filled with endless bluefish action and not a single blue under 10 pounds. I believe

*Capt. Brian Horsley with a fair to middlin'
Outer Banks blue.*

that this "crash," however, is merely a cyclical adjustment akin to a stock market "adjustment" or "hiccup," and is not a result of overfishing or some problem in the ecosystem. Yes, I feel the blues will be back within eight years, maybe less, to the numbers seen when John and I were boys trying to catch girls—and bluefish.

Blues are migratory, both from south to north and back again, and from east to west and back again, ranging clear across the Atlantic into the Mediterranean and Black Sea. Those fish migrating from south to north arrive off Miami in January or so and begin their long journey northwards. They arrive in the Carolinas in April, and in June they are off New York and southern New England. July sees them in the chill Maine waters of the Labrador current, where they stay sometimes into October if the Indian summer is present. The size you catch depends on the school you strike, but for some reason nearly all Maine blues weigh between 10 and 12 pounds. North Carolina's Outer Banks see sporadic runs of even bigger blues that "crash the beach" and cause no small level of pandemonium when they do so.

TACKLE

Because blues vary so greatly in size, and the conditions in which you may find yourself fishing for them are equally divergent, you have to find

Royal Navy survival expert Kevin Garner with an average Maine blue.

out from the local experts what to expect if you will be traveling to find the blues. For instance, inshore blues around Swansboro, North Carolina, run a pound or two, and you can catch a lot of them, too. But surf blues on the Outer Banks can be 16 pounds or more, while Maine blues average about 11 pounds with 16-pound fish possible, though uncommon. Rhode Island and Massachusetts blues run from a few pounds to 15 pounds or so, and Florida blues are generally fairly small. (We don't know for certain how this works. That is, we are unsure whether the blues that arrive off Miami in winter are the same population that arrives in Maine waters come July. What we do know is when they arrive. It may be that the Maine and North Carolina blues are invaders from the eastern Atlantic off the coast of Spain and Portugal, where great runs of huge blues occur.)

Tackle, therefore, has to fit the situation. Snapper blues (the young of the year) need a 6- or 7-weight, tip-flex, 8 1/2- to 9-foot rod. Chopper blues (a few pounds) need more, such as an 8- or 9-weight, tip-flex, 9-foot rod. And the big boys must have at least a 9-weight, tip-flex, 9-foot rod, preferably a 10-weight or even an 11-weight for casting big, wind-resistant flies.

Likewise, the reel has to fit the fish; blues of 7 pounds or more require a decent drag, and double-digit fish demand a drag that can take quite a bit of stress. Reels for big blues also need to have serious line capacity, with at least 200 yards of 30-pound Dacron backing.

Lines, all weight-forward or with a shooting head, can be floating, intermediate, sink-tip, and full-sink. When the blues are crashing the pogies up top, a floater or intermediate is needed. When they are eating the remains immediately after the feeding frenzy or "blitz," a sink-tip is useful. And when they are down deep, cruising and smoking cigars in a rip, a line like Orvis' 600-grain Depth Charge is right. Blues do get down there, like between Maine's Ellingwood Rock and Seguin Island out past the mouth of the Kennebec. Since you don't always know just where the blues are going to be all the time in the water column, you need to have a floater, sink-tip, and fast full-sink with you when you head out.

You can build your own or use a factory-built leader with at least a 40-pound test shock tippet made of braided wire. Bite guards are otherwise required. I prefer a 9- or 10-foot, 20-pound leader with a 50-pound wire tippet.

Flies that are fitting for blues should be large and highly visible. Menhaden imitations are by far what you need most, from 2/0 to 4/0.

TACTICS

Fly-fishing for blues is pretty straightforward. You find the blues and you cast big flies at them. When one eats your fly, you set the hook and hang on.

Well, perhaps it isn't always *quite* that easy to set the hook and bring in the blues, but, sometimes it really is. The best advice is, if you haven't fished a certain area before, to ask other anglers and to follow the other boats out.

Once you get "out there," start watching and smelling for signs of feeding blues. You watch by looking for birds diving or otherwise feeding, and by looking on the surface for signs of menhaden or other bait fish being massacred (blood and fish oil in the water, and floating chunks and pieces of dead menhaden). You smell them by sniffing the air for the scent of the carnage, frankly.

If you can't see any action like this, hit likely looking spots like rips, cuts, just outside the surf zone, and current seams. Sometimes, chumming in a likely looking spot helps get the blues going. It is easy to snag menhaden when they are "schooled up" by casting a large treble hook into the middle of the school and ripping the hook through the water.

I won't try to make this tactics section any more technical or scientific, because it doesn't need to be. Blues just aren't that crafty or difficult to predict, find, and entice into hitting a fly.

Dolphin are next at bat.

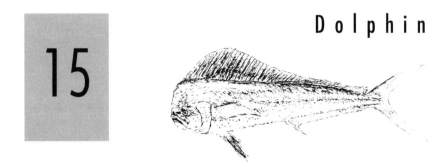

Dolphin

15

Tom Earnhardt
Author of *Fly Fishing the Tidewaters*
Raleigh, North Carolina

Mark Sosin
Executive Editor, *Salt Water Sportsman*
Boca Raton, Florida

George Poveromo
Senior Editor, *Salt Water Sportsman*
Parkland, Florida

Captain Mark Houghtaling
Magic Fingers Fishing Charters
Miami, Florida

THE DOLPHIN IS ONE OF THE MOST TREASURED FISH IN THE SEA. ITS FANTASTIC appearance, with deep blues, brilliant greens, and stunning golds, along with its willingness to eat flies, its accomplished aerobatics, and its reputation for superb table fare, all lead to its popularity.

Inhabiting temperate, subtropical, and tropical waters around the world, the dolphin is seen in ancient art from a variety of civilizations as global as the fish itself. The Hawaiians, Greeks, Polynesians, Phoenicians, and many other societies all enjoyed catching and thriving on these colorful speedsters, and today their numbers are still high.

SEASONS AND SIZES

Check each state's regulations on seasons and sizes for dolphin. You will find that many have no closed season and perhaps even no minimum size limit. However, they probably will have a daily bag limit.

Fly-fishers frequently catch dolphin weighing from a few pounds ("yellowjackets") to monsters like fly-fishing legend Stu Apte's 58-pound behemoth taken in 1964 off Pinas Bay, Panama. Generally speaking, most dolphin caught on the fly weigh somewhere between 5 and 30 pounds, all depending upon your location, the local conditions, the health of the school, luck, your personal skills with the long rod, and many other factors. Keep in mind, however, that although luck is always a factor to *some* degree, it is hard to argue with the knowledge and success of such anglers as Stu (who has held many IGFA records), Mark Sosin, and George Poveromo, whose reputations for finding and catching big dolphin with weird regularity tell the true tale.

Waters that stay warm (in the 70s) throughout the year, as in Florida, have good to excellent dolphin possibilities all the time, but north of Florida the dolphin migrate, following the warmer waters of the Gulf Stream south as cooler temperatures arrive. From the mid-Atlantic coast this means you will find dolphin in blue water (offshore water as opposed to the green water of inshore) as late as September, and in the Gulf Stream right up to November, but then they are out of there. (When the dolphin disappear in November, head for Cabo San Lucas at the tip of Baja California for some of the most outrageous dolphin action in the world. Fish with Grant Hartman, the owner of Baja Anglers right at the marina.) If you are Capt. Mark Houghtaling down in Miami, your best dolphin action is May through August, although Mark points out that they are available all year.

"Yellowjackets" are a nickname for smaller dolphin that travel in schools and are easy targets for the fly rod.

TACKLE

Mark Sosin, a living legend in the field of saltwater angling, loves to chase dolphin with his ever-present Penn and Sage fly rods. Depending on the conditions, he prefers an 8- or 9-weight rod, about 9-feet long, with a quick tip. I agree entirely. However, if you are into some big dolphin, I suggest going to a 10-weight with plenty of backbone for turning the fish and getting it to the boat as soon as possible so that: A) You can safely release it; and B) If you are keeping it, you can get it in and get the fly back in the water for another one. Good choices include the Penn Gold Medal series,

Fly-fishing for dolphin means taking the chance that a wahoo might show up and crash your fly. Your reel must be up to it.

Sage's RPL-X series, and Orvis' Power Matrix rods. Capt. Houghtaling goes with a 9-weight rod.

Your reel must be able to handle extreme runs. True, most of the dolphin you catch will make only short, fast runs, but you must have a reel capable of dealing with both the sudden appearance of a big bull and the occasional attack of a maniacal wahoo. My two favorites are the Orvis Odyssey III and Orvis Battenkill 10/11, but any reel of this caliber will do.

If you go with a reel that has a poor drag system, I guarantee you that sooner or later a hefty dolphin or crazed wahoo is going to smoke it.

Years ago I read an article by Mark Sosin about his affection for simple, common flies, like Deceivers, Bend-Backs, and Clousers, for dolphin (and dozens of other saltwater game fish at that). Naturally, when I got started fly-fishing for dolphin, I tried these three flies, and sure enough, they all worked.

You see, dolphin appear to have very little, if any, preference for anything fancy, including flies. They like anything that appears to be some form of their natural prey, which includes all sorts of bait fish like cigar minnows, filefish, puffers, anchovies, menhaden, flying fish, and many others.

As dolphin are surface fish that stay in the upper layers of the water column, there will be times, especially on very hot days, when they descend to depths of 20 feet or more to find a layer just a bit cooler than the surface water. This is when a fly with lead eyes comes in handy, one that will sink somewhat faster than a similar fly without lead eyes.

Fish holding deep also require a fast sinking line, but the rest of the time you will be well-served with an intermediate line. Weight-forward lines are absolutely the way to go, since offshore breezes are likely in many locales, particularly in the afternoon when the sun has had a chance to warm up the atmosphere and get the old PM wind going. Intermediate lines are used most often by Capt. Houghtaling, who has spent 15 years figuring things out in Miami, so if he says intermediates are what you need, listen to him.

Good dolphin flies and a reel that can take the stress a big bull puts on it are two steps toward success.

Use an 8- to 10-foot leader; start with one capable of handling a 30-pound dolphin, and if you find they aren't that big, then tie on a lighter leader. But be warned: If wahoo are hanging around, or there's a reasonable chance of big bull dolphin, stay with the heavier leader. Capt. Houghtaling suggests a 15-pound tippet with that leader and a 50-pound shock leader to boot.

TACTICS

Perhaps more than for any other saltwater game fish, dolphin tactics revolve around structure. The best advice comes from George Poveromo,

Fred Kluge prepares some menhaden for chumming and chunking along a North Carolina sargassum bed.

who breaks it down into three primary genres: trolling, running and gunning, and chumming and chunking.

Trolling standard lures and natural baits is an excellent way of locating dolphin in scattered patches of sargassum and other surface structure. Once a dolphin is on, keep it on the heavy trolling gear within fly-casting distance of the boat. Yes, *leave it hooked up and in the water.* This technique, which exploits the dolphin's habit of hanging around a hooked friend for reasons unknown to us, is referred to by Tom Earnhardt as the "Judas" technique. You can sight cast to the others or, if they are unseen, cast anyway since they may be just out of your sight but well within sight of your fly. Always leave one fish on until the action dies down, then move on.

Running and gunning is George's term for making high-speed runs between likely looking structure, which might include sargassum on the surface, a tire or board (or some other piece of junk) floating around, current upwellings, or even other boats drifting about. As you *slowly* and *quietly* approach surface structure, check the water beneath for signs of bait fish. If you see no bait fish using the structure, the chances of finding dolphin nearby are substantially reduced. If it looks good, start casting.

Chumming and chunking is my favorite method because I like to have the dolphin come to me and then find a reason to stay there for a while.

Once you locate some good-looking structure, begin tossing small chunks of bait fish in the water, just enough to catch and hold the dolphins' interest. The key is to toss in just enough to keep them hanging around, but not so much that they get full and complacent. You want to *tease* and *excite* them, not *feed* them. A "chum bomb," or a frozen block of fish or fishmeal suspended below the boat also works well, as it slowly releases tiny bits of food as it thaws. Bait fish eat this food and attract dolphin.

You also need to know when to switch flies and how to present those flies when the dolphin begin to get suspicious or be-

We all owe George Poveromo for developing dolphin tactics.

come disinterested. I have found that the most favored colors are yellow, light green, and chartreuse, and that white, gold, and silver are also productive. If the dolphin turn off of these colors, immediately switch to another color. Do not wait more than a few minutes before switching because without something to hold their interest, the dolphin will disappear as fast as they appeared.

Presentation changes are also important. When the fish get funny, radically change your presentation and keep doing so until they turn back on. Still, once their initial interest has fallen off, I find they seldom begin anew with such fervor as during the first run.

Buy binoculars and use them frequently. Binos allow you to see structure, diving birds, and even feeding fish on the surface that your eyes alone would have missed.

Tom Earnhardt points out that a fast sinking line is very important to get your fly down through a layer of small "schoolie" dolphin to the larger dolphin below. Sometimes those larger dolphin can be *much* larger than those you see.

Finally, here's a tactics warning from me. If you are fishing surface structure, especially sargassum, and you see a chunk of the stuff break away from the main mat and start drifting toward your fly, it may be a tripletail heading for your fly. This bizarre fish looks like sargassum and is a great fighter. Be ready!

Red Drum

16

Captain Bramblett Bradham
Bluffton, South Carolina

Captain Harold Carlin
Hatteras, North Carolina

Captain Bill Harris
Atlantic Beach, North Carolina

Captain Rodney Smith
Satellite Beach, Florida

Captain Richard Stuhr
Charleston, South Carolina

THE RED DRUM IS, POUND FOR POUND, ONE OF THE MOST POWERFUL FISH I HAVE ever taken. The first one of any consequence I ever wrestled was with Capt. Rodney Smith in the Banana River Lagoon just south of Cape Canaveral. It weighed about 32 pounds. I knew once I set the hook that I was into something serious, and it took me quite some time and much colorful language to get it into Rodney's broad net.

SEASONS AND SIZES

Reds are available all year throughout their range, from Virginia south all the way around into the Gulf of Mexico along the Texas coast. However, as with most fish, some seasons and conditions are better than others. For instance, late summer days on North Carolina's Pamlico Sound can be great for lots of huge drum, but the best time for bull reds in the Outer Banks surf is an autumn night made miserable with rain and wind. The answer to the riddle for traveling fly-fishers is to call ahead to the local tackle shop for advice.

Red drum can grow to gargantuan proportions, sometimes into the 90-pound range. But while Avon, North Carolina, boasts some of the largest reds available, I believe that future fly-fishing records will continue to come primarily from Florida's Banana River Lagoon and Indian River Lagoon, especially since that state adopted very strict commercial netting rules (see Chapter 25).

TACKLE

Fly rods for red drum start at about an 8-weight; the big bruisers demand 9- and 10-weights. Perhaps the most important feature of a fly rod for big red drum is backbone, as it is critical to constantly put tremendous pressure on the fish as it charges toward oyster beds and other structure able to cut a leader or fly line. Make no mistake about it: An adult bull red will do everything in its power to bend your rod right "to the cork."

The reel must be absolutely flawless when it comes to the drag. Drum make long, very powerful runs again and again, and any drag that doesn't have what it takes won't last long in a protracted fight with a 30- or 40-pound red. You have been warned.

Lines run the gamut from weight-forward floating lines on the flats to intermediates and full sinking lines, all depending on the situation. If you have never fished for reds in a certain area, check with the experts.

Leaders must be abrasion resistant to ward off the knicks

Capt. Rodney Smith, an IGFA record holder, scans the Banana River Lagoon for sign of bull reds.

that oyster beds, barnacles, mangrove roots, and other such things can produce. They should run from about 7 1/2 to 10 feet.

Sharpen the hook on every fly. A drum's mouth can be hard. Always include crab imitations, and a wealth of flies that imitate finger mullet, glass minnows, and mummichogs. A maroon and gold Clouser is one of the most effective red drum flies you can tie on.

TACTICS

Capt. Harold Carlin says if you take the "sheep" attitude while fly-fishing around Hatteras, you won't get into any new water. Says the

Oyster beds require tough leaders.

seasoned angler (who owns the IGFA 16-pound tippet class record for reds), fly-fishers "must also be creative and invent some things for themselves."

Attributing the fishery that is the Outer Banks to nature, he states: "The dynamics of ocean currents, estuaries inlets, Diamond Shoals, and the climate have offered us endless fishing opportunities. Running parallel to the island on the sound side is a shoal we call the reef. It runs the entire length of the island and is a great place to look for smaller reds. Just look for the sloughs and cast the edges, middle, and near the sides. Also, check out the grass lumps; lots of things live there."

Capt. Carlin doesn't mince words when he recommends fly patterns for these Hatteras drum: "Bring your entire selection of flies; you'll need them."

Now, he doesn't mean bring your #28 Adams and similar wets and nymphs. What he means is bring all your *drum* flies, as in shrimp, crab, and bait fish imitations. Have a good range of colors and sizes. Clousers, Deceivers, Bend-Backs, and the like are called for here.

On rods and reels he is more specific and has some definite ideas in mind: "I personally like 8-weights for all the fly-fishing I do except billfish, tuna, and wahoo. I've caught them up to 50 pounds on an 8-weight and it's a blast."

I can personally attest that your 8-weight rod had better be worthy of a big Hatteras drum, because if it isn't you won't have that fish long, and probably not the rod, either. These drum demand reels with a very reliable drag system and plenty of backing.

Here's a chunk of a tale told by Capt. Carlin when he caught his record red drum on April 7th, 1991. It weighed 35 pounds, 8 ounces, and held the 16-pound class tippet for a while:

"We moved slowly in the direction of the nervous water. Once we cut the distance in half it became obvious we had found just what we were after: redfish, hundreds of big, beautiful redfish. We intercepted the school after shutting down the engine and gliding in their direction. The water was dirty around the bed of fish, stirred up by their feeding, but you could still see 3 feet down, and they were stacked up like logs.

"On the second cast I hooked up. The sinking line worked perfectly in getting the fly down among the fish quickly. Now these old drum aren't the fastest of fish, but they ain't slow, either. And strength! Well, imagine a train with a spot on its caboose. After 20 minutes the fish was aboard, weighed, and found to be half a pound shy of the IGFA 16-pound tippet class record. We threw him back in and started looking for the school again.

"Okay, they were moving to the south-southwest again. There

Capt. Bramblett Bradham poles through the spartina flats around Charleston in search of red drum.

was an abrupt change in the color of the water near them. They were moving toward clear water, so I turned the boat and crossed the color change just abreast of where we had just taken one. These drum are very skittish, so there was no way I would get too close to the course I was counting on them to take. I'm here to tell you that just dropping a beer on the deck or waving your arms or fly rod will all too often send them in the opposite direction and down.

"Now we are wired up and ready to make the connection. Lots of talking and planning and rigging was about to be tested. There they were! A large school, now in the clear water, moving slowly and deliberately south. I put the boat back in gear and moved to intercept them. When they got close enough to reach, I zeroed in on a small bunch that was maybe 15 feet closer than the main body, which was only 50 feet away. The first cast landed about 6 feet in front of the smaller group of about eight big reds in crystal-clear water. The leader immediately turned a few degrees and gulped the Deceiver.

"Well, suffice to say that after 25 minutes of a fight that really tested this angler, I got him up close and then brought him in myself. (Mike was fighting his own big drum from the stern.)

"Heaven? Maybe!"

Capt. Rodney Smith hoists Richard Jee's first redfish, a weird Mosquito Lagoon fish that seemed tame and inhaled Richard's fly with a strangely casual attitude.

Capt. Richard Stuhr and Capt. Bramblett Bradham, both Orvis-endorsed guides, are two of South Carolina's hottest drum guides. I know because I have seen them in action and have spent much time fishing with them and picking their considerable brains for every shred of drum advice I could extract. Richard is based out of Charleston where he fishes the Combahee, Edisto, Cooper, Wando, and Ashley River watersheds, and Bramblett was out of Charleston but now guides out of the Hilton Head region; both stress the importance of knowing how the drum are changing their locations and habits as the conditions change. For

Capt. Richard Stuhr releases a tagged red drum.

instance, one day we were staked out with both boats on a mud flat adjacent to a sprawling bed of spartina. The tide was beginning to fall; as it did, the guides expounded on what I was about to see and told me to keep my eyes peeled.

I watched as they talked. The water fell away and the tops of oyster beds began to appear. Soon thereafter, right on cue, barely discernable humps in the water began to materialize in the narrowing channel that funneled the water out of the spartina beds. These humps were the shoulders of red drum meandering out of the spartina into the deeper water of the little channels, where they would take up ambush positions and await the bait fish—mostly finger mullet—they love to dine on. But both Bramblett and Richard also pointed out that crab imitations like McCrabs and Merkins are excellent. The crabs, which drum find irresistable, can be found in the mud and clinging to the oyster piles.

Photo courtesy of Joel Arrington

Black drum often inhabit the same realm as red drum, and they, too, can grow very large, as this Cape Hatteras black drum demonstrates.

Earlier in the day while fishing with Bramblett in the flooded spartina beds, I was keen to learn that it takes some time to learn to spot drum rooting in the shallow water of the flooded grass. Bramblett would see ten drum to my one. But eventually I began to pick up on the technique and soon enough I was spotting many more than I had at the beginning of the lesson. Small pockets of open water that held no grass amid the wavering spartina always held two or three fat drum, and from time to time we would spot one of their tails as the fish went nose-down into the mud to root out a crab. These holes must be approached silently, lest the drum get spooked by the clank of a reel against a cleat or by a loud voice. When a drum hears a foreign noise he knows trouble is afoot and he "blows out" of the hole in a great wooosh, leaving only his wake behind. And when one goes, they all go.

Drum have an excellent sense of smell, a fact that can be exploited by the fly-fisher. One technique I learned from Capt. Rodney Smith was breaking up dead crab bodies and dropping them into areas where drum are known to prowl. The fish pick up the scent and look around for the source. Upon finding it they become all the more likely to start feeding heavily.

Drum move about all their lives. They may or may not move all that far, but they do change locations with the tide every day. They know that bait fish move with the tide, and they simply follow them or head to places where they know the bait fish will be moving through or across. Capt. Bill Harris showed me how to stake out a flat with deep water on one side and spartina on the other in North Carolina's Pamlico Sound, a huge tract of water between the North Carolina mainland and the fabled Outer Banks. He taught me that drum will wait just below the lip of the flat in the deep water, anticipating the bait fish leaving the spartina. Most bait fish won't dawdle on the flat because they feel vulnerable to birds, but they have to go somewhere, so it's into the deep water where they must run the gauntlet of drum.

Bill also told me the tale of what he is sure was an IGFA-record red drum. He was fishing with a well-known flytier and angler who apparently didn't understand the importance of having sharp hooks and setting the hook well when fishing for big reds. Bill spotted a huge school of drum and moved the angler into position. All the fish were big, but as the angler's fly hit the water, a beast of a drum shouldered its way through the crowd and ate the fly. The fight was on.

The angler managed to get the fish near the boat, and Bill could see it was something very special, the drum of a lifetime. The fish surfaced, opened its great maw, and let the fly go.

Bill still talks of this incident and how important sharp hooks are, but he also stresses the importance of being able to find the bigger fish in the first place. It was no accident that Bill found that school that day.

Before we move along, remember that red drum are very susceptible to overfishing. After a famous New Orleans chef released his recipe for "blackened redfish," everyone wanted to eat them, and everyone did. So please, release all, or just about all, of your red drum.

The mighty silver king—the tarpon—is next on our agenda.

17

Tarpon

Captain Les Hill
Tarpon Hunter II Guide Service
Port Charlotte, Florida

Captain Bob Dove
Islamorada, Florida

I VIVIDLY RECALL THE FIRST TIME A TARPON STRUCK MY OFFERING. IT HAPPENED IN a south Florida canal in 1967. I was fishing for bass when the thing attacked, peeling line off the reel and bending the rod with what seemed like terrible anger. The fight lasted perhaps two seconds and scared me for 30 years. I am still scared of tarpon, the mighty "silver king."

Twenty years after that first encounter, I returned to Florida to witness the spectacle of the Gold Coast's Boca Grande Pass, which, along with Charlotte Harbor itself, is Capt. Les Hill's area of operations, a piece of water that is Mecca to tarpon freaks. Untold numbers of giant tarpon stack up like cordwood, and anglers from around the world fish for them with astonishing success. But to be successful you will have to hook many fish, because the hook-to-catch ratio for tarpon is among the highest in the world. Recently I watched a well-known professional bass angler try his hand at Boca Grande tarpon. The poor guy was badly out of his league and lost tarpon after tarpon. Simple mistakes can be avoided if you anticipate the tarpon and use expert skills once the fish is on. Yes, even professional anglers who try hard to appear to know everything when on camera tend to be humbled—as so many anglers do—by the silver king.

The tarpon is special in more ways than just its spirit and strength. It is born offshore from millions of eggs from a single female, looking nothing at all like a tarpon but like a silvery, transparent ribbon. It eventually wanders inshore and undergoes a kind of metamorphosis, reduces its size substantially, and takes on the appearance of a genuine tarpon. It takes approximately seven years to reach maturity at about 4 feet long. It exists upon plankton until about 4 inches long, then begins to feed on bait fish, crabs, and shrimp after it transforms.

Tarpon are warm temperate, subtropical and tropical, inshore and near-shore inhabitants (except when spawning), found from Florida to the lower mid-Atlantic coast and over to Texas. (There is an apparently verified report of a tarpon in the Canadian Maritimes, but such an event was a fluke.) They prefer water temperatures from the upper 70s well into the 80s

This 7-year-old tarpon, although no trophy, is more than a match for many anglers.

and lower 90s, but can tolerate temperatures as low as the mid-60s and as high as 104 degrees.

Tarpon are found on both sides of the Atlantic, with some excellent opportunities along Africa's west coast. The East Coast population tends to be more transient than the Gulf tarpon. The largest ever taken on a fly, caught near Homosassa, Florida, weighed 188 pounds. Speaking of Homosassa, many records and other giant tarpon have been and continue to be caught there, so it is a wise idea to be prepared tackle- and skill-wise.

The aforementioned temperature range gives the tarpon a wide range in the summer months. Great numbers enter North Carolina's Pamlico and Albemarle Sound starting in June, and stay into September to feed on the abundant bait fish—especially menhaden and mullet—and crabs and shrimp. I have stood in a boat with Capt. George Beckwith in the middle of Pamlico Sound and watched what were surely thousands of giant tarpon rolling on the surface and gulping air into their air bladders. They appeared as windshields flashing in the sun—a sight I shall always remember with considerable awe.

Small tarpon are called "ditch" tarpon in Florida because they are often caught in narrow canals that are little more than wide ditches. Those canals can be salt, fresh, or brackish; it doesn't matter to the tarpon because its air bladder allows it to survive under widely varying conditions. Even a small tarpon of 10 pounds is a tremendous challenge, and when you engage one in the tight confines of an old, overgrown canal on an 8-weight rod, you will come away from the contest with shaking arms and a traumatized brain-housing group.

Tarpon are fish not only of the flats, canals, passes, and sounds, but also of the rivers. Throughout its range, it invades rivers and other waterways and often travels far from the sea to eat and carouse. I have found them in the middle of Florida in Leesburg, and come summer they are common in North Carolina rivers like the Neuse. A couple of years ago my friend Rick Pelow hooked into what I suspect was a tarpon in North Carolina's New River, but the beast stripped him clean before he could do anything about it. Capt. Lee Manning, aboard his charter boat, the *Nancy Lee III*, has seen pods of tarpon cruising the beach between the New River Inlet and Bogue Inlet, and every now and then a North Carolina pier angler catches a tarpon, and these fish are often quite large.

SEASONS AND SIZES

Tarpon do not vary in size with the season and location nearly as much as game fish like stripers. In regions like south Florida and the Keys, a flyfisher can strike a 120-pound tarpon at any time in many different situations. However, there are regions where the fish tend to be in the same size category, such as Pamlico Sound, where most of the tarpon weigh 70–90 pounds, and no juvenile fish are reported.

Seasons are important, but more important in some regions than others. For example, tarpon from Georgia to North Carolina are fish of late spring and summer, perhaps early fall in Georgia. But south of Cape Canaveral and Tampa, they can be found at any time of year, although early spring is when the tarpon fishing really starts to get hot. The rivers and canals from central Florida on down hold tarpon in winter. The Florida Keys have resident tarpon throughout the year, but April through June are the best months.

TACKLE

Tarpon tackle must be flawless, the best there is. There is no margin of error in fighting one, and your tackle can have no margin of mediocrity.

Rods for ditch tarpon can start at an 8-weight, but such a rod is risky. Ten-weights to 13-weights are preferable, with the backbone to drive a hook into a tarpon's notoriously hard mouth and keep it there during a wild fight including numerous repeated jumps that find the fish 12 feet in the air again and again, spinning, tumbling, thrashing, and shaking. The lengths start at 8 feet and go to 11 feet or thereabouts, although I think an 11-foot rod is too long and unnecessary. I believe a 9-foot, 12-weight rod with tremendous striking power is best for tarpon over 50 pounds, but an 8-foot, 8-weight is acceptable for ditch tarpon provided they are in confined waters and can't bolt to open water like the big guys in the channels and flats can.

Tarpon reels can get pretty expensive, that is, if you want a tarpon reel that can actually handle a tarpon. Abel, Sage, Billy Pate, Orvis, and like names make reels with drags that can deal with the tyrannical tarpon, which will deal severely with anything less than a perfect drag. I have seen lesser reels seize and explode under the awesome power of the tarpon, drags fused and mangled. Line capacities have got to be serious, with 250 yards of backing being standard. It also helps if the reel is a multiplier for taking up line fast when a tarpon rushes the boat.

UV-resistant floating and intermediate weight-forward or shooting-head lines are needed for many situations, but you must also have a sink-tip. Tarpon live in sun country, remember, and ultraviolet light breaks down PVC (polyvinyl chloride), which coats modern fly lines. Be sure to use a line no shorter than 85 feet in order to reach tarpon without spooking them; 100-foot lines are even better.

Leaders are equally special. It is very easy for a tarpon to break off using his armored head covered with large scales, and the gill plate is especially dangerous to a leader. The same day I saw that bass pro lose tarpon after tarpon, I watched one of the most respected fly-fishers in the world, Stu Apte, perform a "Keys release" on a large tarpon he had been fighting for a while. The fly line was through the tiptop when the tarpon turned to one side and caught the leader under his gill plate, and he was gone. Stu, being Stu, didn't bat an eye and was genuinely glad the tarpon had broken itself off at that point. Stu said in Florida Keys tarpon tournaments that would have passed for a caught-and-released fish, since the line was through the tiptop. I don't fish Keys tournaments, or any tournaments for that matter, but to me the idea that a fish lost at the side of the boat is actually a caught fish is, of course, ridiculous. But this way the tarpon need not be handled, often a good thing provided the fish isn't completely exhausted. An exhausted tarpon— any fish—released without being revived is likely to die.

I prefer to go with Lefty Kreh's standard system of building a leader, the descending one-half system. The mid-section is about one-half as long as the butt, and if you need to add additional sections between the butt and the tippet, each is one-half as long as the section above it. For big tarpon in water that isn't particularly clear (you may have to double the length of the butt for nervous tarpon in gin-clear water), start with a 6-foot butt section of 40- to 50-pound test. Then go to a 36-inch section of 20- to 25-pound test. A shock tippet comes next, and it must be very heavy and straight. It should be 12–18 inches long and test at 80–100 pounds. (**Warning:** If you

*Long, accurate casts are a must when stalking nervous tarpon
in quiet shallows.*

are into IGFA records, or just want to be prepared in case the *big one* does
show up behind your fly, the tippet can be no longer than 12 inches.
Remember that!) This gives you a 10- to 10 1/2–foot leader that will turn
the big fly over and have the capacity to drive the hook home, plus reduce
the chance of being broken off by the tarpon's gill plate or rough mouth. I
should stress here that having a stiff, abrasion-resistant, straightened shock
tippet is important—critical, in fact.

Tarpon flies can run from the standard Stu Apte Tarpon Fly, Keys guide
Steve Huff's Tarpon Fly, Chico Fernandez Tarpon Fly, Whistler, and Sea-
Ducer, to some very effective custom flies. Sizes generally go from 2/0 to
4/0, but plenty of tarpon have been caught on smaller and bigger flies.

TACTICS

The tarpon is infamous for surprise attacks. Many Florida anglers walk
around with a stunned look on their face because of a sudden, unexpected,
and very violent encounter with a deranged tarpon, and I am one of them.
So is Capt. Rodney Smith, but Rod is so cool that he has learned to hide the
expression. Despite this insidious proclivity for well-laid ambushes, tarpon
are quite predictable.

Guides and other tarpon fanatics learn to pattern tarpon: They know when tarpon will move from one area to another and they go to choke points to intercept them, such as a narrow cut between flats and a deep-water channel over which a bridge is situated. They also know that the flats hold tarpon, and these flats are considered by nearly all tarpon nuts to be the classic tarpon fly-fishing situation. And the fact that tarpon feed heavily at night is not lost upon them.

There are two primary thoughts when it comes to finding tarpon: Look in the areas you know or suspect they will be traveling through when relocating, and hunt them in areas that hold fish for hours at a time as opposed to being highways or back-alley shortcuts. Some spots can be both. Spending time on the water is the answer to figuring all this out.

For the flats and any other situation that allows sight fishing, stealth is usually vital. Visible tarpon are naturally wary because of the conditions: They know their situation puts them at a disadvantage when it comes to a predator. A long, accurate cast is called for, along with a quiet approach to put you in a position where stripping the fly away from the tarpon is possible. Quartering-away retrieves are often just the ticket. Your position in relation to the wind, and your ability to lay the fly where you want it without spooking the tarpon when the fly line lands on the water, are paramount to success. The fly must not land too close to the tarpon because it will scare him. The same is true if your position in re-

A lap full of muscle and attitude

lation to the tarpon forces you to bring the fly toward the fish—it will probably scare him off.

In stained water, like that found in busy channels and canals, the fly-fisher need not worry so much about the tarpon seeing him, but stealth is still demanded. Be wary of noises in the boat—as you always are—and accidentally jumping a tarpon you didn't see, a great boil of tea-colored water marking the fish's churning departure.

When working a school of tarpon in deep water, where the tarpon are moving down on bottom but individual fish are coming to the surface to gulp air, you must think ahead. Oftentimes *far* ahead if you are going to be successful. This is a game of estimates. You estimate how fast the school is traveling and how far you have to get ahead of them to get the fly down to their level in such a way that you can strip away from them once they see it. Timing has to be perfect. Start by just watching to see how much distance is covered between rolling tarpon. Now you can estimate the school's speed down below. Go well out around them—it's better to get way ahead and have to wait for them than it is to risk spooking the school—and cast back toward the school. Strip when you believe they are approaching the fly and are within striking distance.

But when do you start to strip when you can see the tarpon or when you have a good idea where it is? The general rule practiced by most guides and other tarpon specialists is when the fly is no closer than 5–6 feet and no further away than 10–12 feet.

Schools of tarpon can be more difficult to work. If at all possible, cast so that the lead tarpon does not see the fly, but one of the fish behind it does. This way you won't spook the entire school if the tarpon cuts and runs because he saw the boat or you. If the lead fish follows the fly, the whole school will follow, and if the lead fish spooks, the jig is up because the whole school is going to scatter right along with that lead fish. Your guide will tell you all this, that is, if they are professionals like Les Hill and Bob Dove, but you are going to have to remind yourself when you are out alone.

Tarpon enjoy lurking near mangroves because of the prolific forage. This is great when it comes to attracting and holding tarpon in one area, but you have the additional challenge of keeping the irate tarpon out of the roots, which sometimes can seem impossible. A high-modulus rod and super tough leader, and the nerve to put the rod to the fish and manhandle it away from the maze of roots, will put more tarpon at your feet. Many anglers have difficulty putting immense pressure on the tarpon to turn him away from trouble, but if you watch the experts you will see rods bent "to the corks" and the angler's body twisting away from the tarpon. *Put the pressure to the fish.*

There is another flats resident you simply must try. He is the "gray ghost," also known as the bonefish.

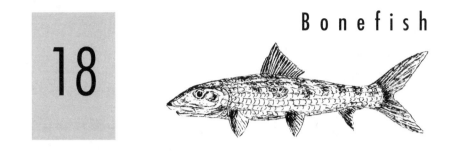

18

Bonefish

Mark Sosin
Executive Editor, *Salt Water Sportsman*
Boca Raton, Florida

I NEVER SEE MARK SOSIN FOCUS SO INTENTLY AS HE DOES ON BONEFISH. WHEN HE spies one and decides it is worth a cast, everything else in and around him seems to fade to black as he brings his entire being on line to try to fool this remarkable game fish, the "gray ghost" of the flats. When he gets within casting range, only he and the bonefish exist: It is *mano a bone-o,* and no one and nothing else matters except the contestants. This is what bonefish do to people.

Comparable to a silver Ferrari blasting through a pool of mercury, the bonefish is to the flats what the cheetah is to the Serengeti Plain: nothing is sleeker, nothing is craftier, and nothing even *thinks* it is in its class when it comes to maneuverability and outright awesome speed.

Found from southern Florida south, and one of the most popular game fish in the Florida Keys, the bonefish is the nervous Nellie of the flats, ready to panic and flee at the slightest sound, vibration, or any other impetus that makes it feel threatened. Because it is preyed upon by sharks and barracuda that prowl the flats where it hunts for crustaceans and mollusks (primarily the former), the bonefish has developed its protective camouflage and tremendous speed to go along with its fear of everything. (If you ever have the opportunity to see a barracuda stalk and strike a bonefish, you will always remember it. I liken it to matter and antimatter coming together: the result is sudden and spectacular, and over in a second.) This makes the bonefish the great challenge that it is. Still, it is approachable if you use your head and are silent, for sometimes even the most paranoid game fish in the sub-tropics and tropics becomes so intent on feeding that it forgets something—or someone—may be looking for it.

SEASONS AND SIZES

Bonefish are prone to being put off the bite when a cold snap piles in, and the Keys are certainly prone to cold snaps in the winter. Guides there

The flats boat allows the fly-fisher to cover more water and therefore affords him the chance to locate more bonefish.

have learned to find and fish flats that warm the most during a cold snap, but even this can be hard fishing. Therefore, the bones of spring, summer, and early fall are more likely to be eating. Still, look for a dark flat during a cold snap, because, as opposed to a light-colored flat, the dark flat will be a few degrees warmer—it holds the heat of the sun rather than reflect it back. (This is the same principle as finding winter trout holding in deep holes adjacent to a dark mud flat.) Turtle grass covering a flat may make the flat darker or it may be that the bottom itself is simply a darker sand.

Bones can grow to 19 pounds, but most will weigh from 3 pounds or so to 7 or 8 pounds. Anything bigger is a nice fish, and double-digit bonefish are special. For trophy bonefish, Islamorada in the Keys is your best bet. Like Homosassa for big tarpon, Islamorada, for some reason, produces more big bones that any other major sportfishing port.

TACKLE

Small bonefish can be handled in exciting battles with a rod as light as a 5-weight, generally speaking. I say "generally speaking" because there are some kooks running around the Keys who like to go after these speedsters

A dark bottom will warm the water better than a light one. The grass on the bottom behind this bonefish helps hold the heat from the sun.

with rods much lighter, just for the thrill. As long as your ability to play the fish is up to it, and by this I mean you can still get the bonefish in fast enough for a safe release, then go for it. But be warned: If a shark or barracuda sees the bonefish struggling—and the longer you fight the bone the better the chances of a predator species taking issue with it—you could have a problem. I've seen a pretty 2-weight popped by the impact of a giant barracuda ramming a 10-pound bone in mid-play. The rod had cost $500. The fly-fisher, being ethical, did not send the rod back to the company, which would have replaced it with no questions asked, because he knew he was responsible for its destruction and not a flaw in workmanship. He grimaced and beared it, then promptly reached under the gunnel to the recessed rod holder and pulled out an Orvis Superfine 1-weight. Yes, the man is truly demented.

A 7- or 8-weight, tip-flex rod that is 9 feet long is an excellent choice for most bonefish situations. Some fly-fishers prefer a slightly shorter rod that is mid-flex, but that's a personal choice and certainly a reasonable one.

Bonefish reels must have outstanding drags, because the bonefish is absolutely going to give it a test run. Actually, the bonefish is going to give it several test runs, one right after the other, and those runs might be from 50 to 100 yards long and very frightening. Never short-change yourself with a so-so reel on the bonefish flats.

Lines used for bonefish are almost always floating weight-forward, and should be resistant to UV rays.

Leaders are generally about 9 feet in length. I like a knotless leader, 12- to 16-pound test. A short, but not too heavy, shock leader *may* be necessary when fishing a flat with young mangroves growing up in it.

Bonefish flies supposedly imitate little creatures bonefish eat. I question whether many are genuine imitations, however, and feel that most exploit the bonefish's instinct of scooting forward to eat something that looks like it was about to get away. Exceptions are crab and shrimp patterns. Classic bone flies are the always-popular Crazy Charlie (there are a host of variations on this pattern), Merkin Crab, McCrab, Horror, and Snapping Shrimp, but you will find that many Keys guides tie their own specialty flies and claim they are better than any generic pattern. I doubt this, too, but would be willing to return to the Keys again and fish—*gratis*, of course—with any guide who is sure his patterns are superior.

TACTICS

Crafty bonefish tactics are a must, that is, if you want lots of big bones. There's a lot more to hunting bones than there is to hunting bluegills and seatrout, I assure you. The pros have developed tactics that without a doubt put them onto more and bigger bones than those fly-fishers who just plod along the flats casting to distant *tailing* fish and *muds*. The best guides and professional anglers like Mark Sosin are intimately familiar with the flats and they know the prey.

They know that the banded snapping shrimp (*Alpheus armillatus*) is the major forage species for bones, and they use flies they often tie themselves that imitate this most important shrimp. Patterns can appear different because the banded snapping shrimp can have a body of dark green, brownish orange, brown, greenish tan, greenish brown, light brown, and dark gray. It has nine bands on the body (twice the number of bands are on the abdomen as on the carapace) that also vary in color from dark to pearly white, and it has whitish bands on yellowish orange legs. The shrimp grows to slightly more than an inch and a half. A fly tied to exactly match the color phase of the banded snapping shrimp being eaten on a certain flat can be highly effective, as can one tied to match the Atlantic palolo worm (*Eunice fucata*).

This worm, which can hatch in spectacular numbers in the Keys from May to July, has a brownish-red color to its 1 1/2-inch body. Although it is more important to the tarpon, bonefish do feed heavily on them when they hatch. A simple fly tied to imitate them can be amazingly productive.

Bonefish are stalked. The three primary methods of finding them are looking for the tips of the tails protruding from the water as they feed on the flat (*tailing*), looking for small patches of water on a calm surface that look rougher than the surrounding water (nervous water), and looking for clouds of mud on the flat (*muds*) formed as the bonefish roots on the bottom for a bite to eat.

Tailing fish may be single fish out and about on their own, or there may be several fish there. Assume there are several and that you can't see them all; I have seen many flyfishers not consider that they might not be able to see all the bone-

The right stalk will reward you.

fish in a school (or that there even *was* a school) and spook the fish because they dropped the line right over one's back or put the fly too close to a fish. When one blows out, they all blow out, and you will have to locate another school.

Nervous water indicates that something is just below the surface. If you watch you will see the water moving, indicating in what direction the fish making it are moving. Determine how fast the fish are moving and make a cast in front of them, but keep in mind that, as in any bonefish situation, a bit too far in front of the fish is better than too close.

When you find a mud, you can tell whether the bonefish are still there by considering the density of the suspended particles in the cloud. Usually, the denser the cloud the fresher the cloud. However, some types of bottom will hang suspended longer than others, and you have to learn to tell the

Mark Sosin with a classic bonefish. Mark, who is responsible for a large chunk of the saltwater angling information we have today, is known for going out of his way to help others catch more fish.

difference between a cloud of mud created by bonefish and one made by a stingray that just took off. The latter will often have a streak running away from the main cloud indicating the route the ray took. Muds are created when the bonefish squirts a stream of water from its mouth into the bottom to uncover a crab or some other tasty tidbit that it suspects is hiding thereabouts. When you see the resulting cones on the bottom, you know bones have been there. The fresher the cone (more clearly defined edges) the more recently the bonefish passed by. Yes, you can actually track bonefish.

Stalking requires polarized sunglasses to cut through the glare on the water and reduce stress on the eyes, a brimmed hat (perhaps one with some neck protection, too), and sunscreen or a long-sleeved shirt. The hat and sunglasses are important because just seeing the bonefish is half the battle. Many fly-fishers are amazed the first time they fish for bones with a guide because the guide sees so many—sometimes all—of the fish long before the fly-fisher does. Smart guides know to keep the sun at right angles to the fly-fisher, which eliminates glare directly in front of the fly-fisher.

Once a tail or mud is spotted, the stalk begins. It is of the utmost importance to remain silent and unseen during the stalk, which means you may have to get down on one knee or at least bend over to lower your profile. Many casts to bones will be made from a kneeling or bent-over position, so practice making casts of 30 to more than 50 feet from these positions.

Gently lay the fly a few feet in front of the bonefish and, unless the bone jumps it immediately, lift it off the bottom as the fish approaches to simulate a shrimp or something trying to escape. You will see the bonefish scoot forward to eat the fly, and you will feel a fairly firm bump when it hits the fly.

Consider also the tide. Unlike snook fishing that is often best on a falling tide in an inlet, bonefish feed more heavily on a rising tide on a flat. The contradiction is simple: Snook post themselves in the inlet to catch the bait fish coming down from upriver as water levels fall, whereas bonefish prefer the incoming tide because the rising water allows them access to areas where crabs, mollusks, and tiny bait fish have been safe since the water fell far enough to move the bonefish out.

On the falling tide, Mark will focus attention on a flat's drainage pattern, which is determined by nearly indiscernible channels in the flat. The bonefish will often get in these slight, elongated depressions to catch the creatures being swept off the flat as the water falls.

Since we are on the flats, let's look for some barracuda.

19

Barracuda

Mark Sosin
Executive Editor, *Salt Water Sportsman*
Boca Raton, Florida

I VIVIDLY RECALL ONE OF THE MOST MEMORABLE BARRACUDA ATTACKS I EVER witnessed. It happened while fishing off the coast of North Carolina one July. We were anchored over a wreck, enjoying some very good amberjack action, with the occasional dolphin and king mackerel showing up to add to the fun.

A 7- or 8-pound amberjack was about to be gaffed at the bow when a giant barracuda materialized just below the surface at the stern and, seeing the thrashing jack at the bow, shot like a streak of lightning toward the doomed fish, covering the 50 feet between the stern and bow in about one second.

The 6-foot-long 'cuda struck the hapless fish immediately behind the head and never slowed down. It sliced through the jack as if it had one of those Jedi knight light sabers Luke Skywalker and Darth Vader used in *Star Wars*. With the weight of the fish suddenly reduced by two-thirds, the pressure the angler had been putting on the jack caused the fish's bloody head to fly out of the water and go sailing over the angler's head to land on the deck behind him.

The barracuda was never seen again.

This incident is typical of the great barracuda's attitude and abilities. The fish is a genuine killing and eating machine with a set of impressive dental work the likes of which comparatively few fish can boast about and whom nearly all are terrified of. (The African tigerfish has equally impressive teeth and then some.) The great barracuda is the hit man of the Atlantic.

SEASONS AND SIZES

The great barracuda inhabits the temperate, subtropical, and tropical seas, preferring water temperatures starting in the low 70s. In North America the only year-round barracuda action is south of Cocoa Beach and

Tampa, Florida, but cold snaps can put the fish off the bite during the winter months.

Key West has been the site for all but one of the IGFA fly-fishing records for barracuda; the other one was set out of Marathon Key. Florida Key 'cudas are extremely common and can grow very large, but boating an especially big 'cuda on fly-fishing tackle is intimidatingly prohibitive. Countless times throughout the year fly-fishers hook huge barracuda, but most break off. The problem is, of course, their legendary teeth coupled with sizzling runs and absolute brute strength. If you can get a 30-pound barracuda to the boat with 30-pound tippet, you have done well. Imagine the challenge of fly-fishing for these heathens with 6- or 8-pound tippet!

But get this: Great barracuda can reach weights of 90 pounds plus. Even I have a hard time imagining the battle that would take place with a 'cuda of this size—or even 30 pounds less, for that matter—particularly if the fish was still "green" (not at all tired) at the gunnel. I do know this: The fish would never be allowed in my boat. A quick and safe release at the gunnel would be the *only* way to go with an aquatic chain saw like that.

TACKLE

If you are intentionally targeting big barracuda on the fly for the first time, start with a bare minimum of a stiff 9-weight (max modulus here, boys and girls) and you should almost certainly go heavier. If you are experienced at dealing with them, large 'cudas can be handled with a mid-flex, rod. I often use a 9-foot, 12-weight Orvis Saltrodder that weighs 6 1/2 ounces and has a full wells grip. Normally my tarpon rod, it works well on hefty, grumpy barracuda.

Warning: If you are fly-fishing in the Keys for permit, pompano, bones, and the like with traditional rods for those fish, watch for prowling barracuda that enjoy nothing better than hitting your fish as you play it and stripping your reel of every inch of line and backing, and sometimes even popping the rod before you can say, "What the . . ."

The reel must be first class in the drag department. Any skipping will likely break the fish off. A drag not up to par in endurance will combust. Have at least 250 yards of 30-pound backing available.

Leaders should be wire. Although you can use and get away with (sometimes) using a heavy mono shock tippet, wire is the way to go because you lose far fewer flies and the wire does not seem to put the 'cuda off at all. A 10-inch wire leader rated to 50 pounds is fine.

A barracuda fly might be any fly, but elongate flies like extended Deceivers, Big Eye Spearing (which probably look like needlefish to the

Typical barracuda flies.

barracuda), and the Afternoon Delight, as well as wide flies like a Mikane Special or Bunker, are most productive. If streamers don't interest them, tie on a large slider. Be prepared to switch flies often because barracuda teeth will destroy even the toughest fly. It's a trade-off, I suppose.

A good, long hook remover of some kind is required. Use a gaff through the mouth, too.

Do not hold the barracuda in the water with your hands when releasing it. Another barracuda under the boat may think your hands wrapped around the barracuda's body look like an easy meal. Instead, resuscitate the fish with the gaff in its mouth. When the fish starts getting antsy, quickly pull the gaff free.

TACTICS

This is where Mark Sosin shines; the man has it down pat.

Mark seems to enjoy flats barracuda action most because he sight fishes for the things. He spots a big 'cuda, which I have heard him call "telephone poles" for the way they appear as dark poles in the clear, shallow water of a flat, and then works the line out. He stresses that you want the fish to come to the fly, so don't bring the fly right to the fish. Barracuda are

Nice teeth, eh? The barracuda is a sucker for teasing, but those teeth can cut you, the teaser fish, and you again if you're not careful.

ferocious predators used to forage fish keeping their distance; fish (flies) don't just wander in close proximity to the business end of a barracuda. Therefore, Mark puts the fly well away but still within sight of the fish, then he begins an erratic, fast retrieve. This is what the 'cuda expects a potential meal to do when it has been seen, and such a retrieve often triggers the fish's instinctive kill-and-eat response.

It happens with shocking abruptness. The "telephone pole" goes from zero to warp speed in less than a Marine drill instructor's heartbeat, slamming into the fly as if it was suspected of taking liberties with the 'cuda's sister. Mark emphasizes not setting the hook until you feel the weight of the fish; I can personally attest to how easy it is to panic and set the hook (with a full body twist to the side) before the barracuda has the fly in its mouth.

It is of the utmost importance to be sure any fly line lying on the deck is free and clear. The fish is going to bolt, and if the line is hung on something the game will be over as quickly as it started.

Get the fish on the reel fast. You will *not* be stripping this fish in.

Barracuda jump. If you watch Mark play one on a fly rod, he bows to the fish as it jumps just as if it were a tarpon, and he anticipates the jump. As soon as the fish hits the water Mark's hand is back on the handle, ready to reel. But he is also ready to let the fish run again.

Besides the flats where bonefish play, barracuda are found hanging over, in, or beside structure. Wrecks, rocks, buoys, reefs, boats, and piers all attract barracuda, which hunt by ambush.

I recall reading as a boy about a lady walking her poodle along a southern Florida marina pier one fine day. The little dog wanted to play, so she tossed a stick or something into the water and Fifi dutifully bounded down the pier and launched herself into the water.

Little Fifi never knew what hit her.

The barracuda hiding beneath the pier shot out and instantly cut the dog in half. It was gone as quickly as it had appeared.

Smaller barracuda tend to swim in schools, sometimes numbering in the hundreds. It can be frustrating trying to get at the larger fish hanging beneath a school, but chumming and teasing can bring the big ones up to you. A chum block suspended below the boat will draw small bait fish, while chunks about the size of your thumb will draw larger fish like yellowtail snapper. The feeding action of the bait fish, snapper, and smaller barracuda will stir the larger ones below, but oftentimes you need to encourage the big guys with a teaser right on the surface.

One man catches a snapper and hooks it through the back. On a stout spinning rod, he suspends the snapper so that it is frantically swimming on the surface. Sharp eyes are needed to pull the snapper out of the water as

This young barracuda will likely stick close to home, even after release.

the smaller barracuda attack. With the snapper continuing to make a commotion on the surface and the little guys always missing, the big 'cuda will often come barreling toward the surface to catch and eat the upstart snapper. The snapper is pulled away just in the nick of time, which will infuriate the big 'cuda. The snapper is lowered again and the same trick is performed. Now the fly is cast in and worked on the surface beside the snapper that has once again been lowered to the surface. As the 'cuda attacks the snapper, it is quickly withdrawn, but the fly is left. Usually the barracuda will immediately strike the fly in retaliation and frustration.

To further raise the ire of a trophy barracuda, slap the surface with a rod tip a few times to simulate bait fish being attacked. Rapidly swish the tip back and forth several times in the water, too, creating bubbles and sound that the barracuda come to investigate, again thinking something is being chased and eaten.

Great barracuda aren't nomadic; they'll take up residence on a certain piece of structure or on a certain flat and stay there until the food runs out. This means that if you miss a big one on Monday, you can come back on Tuesday and likely still find it there.

Barracuda don't require the cunning involved with catching other more sophisticated game fish like permit. You simply have to trip their trigger, and you do that by playing upon their predator instincts.

Now comes the fabulous snook.

20

Snook

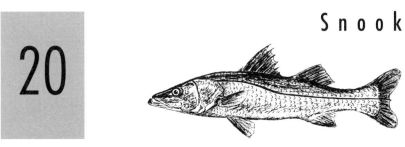

Captain Rodney Smith
Satellite Beach, Florida

RICK PELOW AND I WERE WORKING A NARROW, MANGROVE-LINED CANAL ON Florida's Sanibel Island in late December, 1994. With me in the stern—a place I was very familiar and comfortable with—the canoe barely moved forward down the board-straight canal; I didn't want to spook the snook I knew just had to be hiding in the roots of the mangroves. We were the only ones in the canal, which looked perfect for the fabled game fish. As it was winter, I figured the snook would be there.

A slight splash about 40 feet ahead got my attention and I told Rick to fire at it. He did, and the snook exploded instantly, Rick's rod bending under

Large snook from the beach are tremendous fun. Know where and when to find them, then match what they are eating.

the wild gyrations of the young fish. But Rick was ready for the snook's antics, and a couple of minutes later it surrendered at the side of the canoe. We took its picture, revived it, and sent it on its way back into the labyrinth of roots. We enjoyed three more snook out of that cramped little canal.

For such little guys, like tarpon they put every ounce of their being into the fight. These were Rick's first snook, and to be honest, I hadn't fished for them since 1967 in a little canal near the Ft. Lauderdale airport where we were crabbing with Richard and Ronny Bright. It brought back some fine memories.

Paddling that canoe down the canal, my memories came flooding back to me, of strong game fish with muscular sides and a prominent, single, black stripe running from its gill plate to its tail. Unfortunately Rick had the bothersome tendency to quickly surpass me in skills that had taken me decades to procure. Actually, I killed him and sank his body in the canal as a kind of inshore artificial reef. He never saw the paddle coming.

But that was then and this is now, and the snook are still there in that silent, narrow, wonderful canal on Sanibel Island, as they are in so many backwaters, surf zones, and shadowy bridge-covered channels where anglers hope to entice them with feather and steel.

SEASONS AND SIZES

Seasons for snook revolve around water temperatures, as they are sub-tropical and tropical fish. You won't find them in any great numbers much north of Florida, as they prefer water temperatures in the 70s and 80s, even 90s. When the water drops below 65, snook start to get uncomfortable; 60 degrees is nearly dangerous for them.

Snook of a pound or so are often as commonplace as bream, but you have to try harder for trophy fish. Places like Sebastian Inlet and the 10,000 Islands region of southern Florida are known to produce out-standing snook, but to limit these fish to those regions would be wrong. The truth is, big snook are caught throughout coastal, central, and south Florida.

TACKLE

The snook you pursue will dictate the tackle you use. While rods should be in the 9-foot range, actions can vary. In mangroves a tip-flex, high-modulus rod is needed to horse the powerful snook away from the roots, but in channels with nonthreatening structure and in the surf, a mid-flex rod is

Fly-fishing wizard Mark Sosin, host of Mark Sosin's Saltwater Journal, *displays a giant snook caught on a fly. Mark has been a leader in taking trophy saltwater game fish on fly tackle for 30 years.*

suitable provided the wind isn't too much and the flies aren't exceptionally big. Weights start at a 7-weight for juvenile snook and go to a 10-weight for big bruisers.

Whereas an adult snook is quite strong and resolute in freeing itself of the fly, it is not as strong as a bonefish or tarpon. Snook can grow to more than 50 pounds, and fly-fishers regularly take them in the 10- to 20-pound category.

A 20-pound snook is a devil to fight. It will jump, thrash, peel line off the reel with sudden spurts of energy, wrap your line around any structure it can find, and in general make an exciting nuisance of itself. Your reel and drag have to be quality to handle the scorching runs.

Weight-forward, floating, intermediate, sink-tip, and full-sink lines round out a complete selection of snook lines. Conditions can change rapidly, so you really do need them for moving from location to location in a boat. You will use the full-sink line least, by far, but it can come in handy in heavy current for snook that are holding down a ways. However, in the mangroves or surf, a floating or intermediate line may be all you need. Tropical lines that are resistant to the sun's line-damaging UV rays will increase the life of your line.

Leaders have to be abrasion-resistant and are best made by you. A heavy butt section is needed for large snook that want large flies, and the leader should be at least 10 feet long. A 12-inch, 30-pound-test shock tippet will help ward off the rough bridge abutments and mangrove roots.

Juvenile snook are known to quickly jump on just about any fly. Big snook have grown wise and persnickety, so if you want a big one you will probably have to use a fly that mimics the grunt or whatever forage fish the adult snook is hunting at the time.

Young snook are easily fooled by glass minnow imitations and small Deceivers and Clousers from 1 to 2/0. Crab imitations and flies that mimic shrimp are also excellent, and a 2/0 Muddler Marabou jerked on the surface is difficult for a 3-pound snook to pass up. Bigger snook can easily handle a 4/0 fly, and I have seen tarpon anglers take them with 6/0 flies. Your flies should range in color across the spectrum so that you can match whatever the snook are feeding on. Don't go out with one or two patterns and think you are all set to handle whatever comes your way.

TACTICS

Small snook will infest the upper reaches of canals—salt, brackish, and fresh—and estuaries that provide a lot of cover for them to hide and hunt

Charlotte Harbor and the surrounding estuaries and inlets make excellent snook habitat, as Capt. Les Hill's anglers can attest.

The snook of summer are beach fish.

in. Don't think that water appearing more suited to bream, bass, and catfish won't hold snook.

Agricultural drainage ditches and flood control ditches can hold a lot of snook, which feed on the many minnows and bream that inhabit these reaches.

Young snook just aren't that smart, and they can be seen and heard from a ways away, smacking bait fish and tearing up the surface. They will hit a nice variety of flies worked on the surface or just under, and they don't require a fly to simulate anything in particular; if it looks good, they will eat it. But be warned that adult snook sometimes hunt right beside the young ones in confined backwaters. You must be ready for whatever shows up.

Adult snook are another matter. Start your hunt by thinking about the tide. At river mouths and inlets, cast a 3/0 Deceiver tied to mimic the predominant bait fish as the high tide begins to run out. The falling tide is a tool: it brings tens of thousands of bait fish that were upriver into one area, and the snook know this. They will post themselves in the mouth or inlet and ambush the bait fish as they come by, feeding heavily at night as well as during the day.

Be cautious when working clear water because snook have excellent eyesight at any age. However, young snook aren't as easily put down as adults because they have yet to learn that the silhouette of a human means trouble. A quiet approach and the longest cast possible help not to scare snook, and use caution in your presentation as well as the selection of fly. A loud splash in clear water near a snook could startle it, and too big a fly worked too aggressively will often have a similar result.

Retrieve the fly quickly in most situations—you don't want the snook to get a really good look at it. You want to prey on his predatory instincts, particularly the one that says, "There's a sardine going by! It's trying to escape! Eat it!" This is different from sight casting to tarpon, when you want the tarpon to see the fly and chase it with growing interest and anger.

Snook are transitional game fish. You will find them in great numbers from spring through the summer in the surf and near jetties, but in the fall and winter they will move to the warmer waters of rivers and canals. When they are relocating between seasonal grounds you can make good guesses where they will be feeding, and such places always revolve around structure of some sort. Bridges with lots of pilings, shoals, oyster beds, rocks, jetties, marinas, seawalls, docks, piers, and drainage pipes are all snook habitat because of the myriad bait fish that can gather around the structure.

Because snook have definite temperature preferences, you can predict where they are going to be. For instance, in January and February focus your attention on narrow, inland canals, creeks, and rivers. Here snook gather in large numbers to enjoy the warmest water they can find, but forage can be a problem because the amount of prey doesn't always suit the number of snook in one area. This makes your fly a prime target. A few winters ago while I was fishing with Rod, he pointed out some young mangroves growing on an island in the Banana River Lagoon. He said that that spot can be excellent for snook in spring and fall, but in the winter they are farther upriver, so we would be wasting our time there if we were to hit it then. Little tidbits of info like that can make all the difference.

Chumming can be deadly effective on snook. Pilchards and other bait fish tossed live into a chum slick really get the snook anxious. It is always advisable to have a cast net along, and to know how to use it.

If you have flats—hopefully lined with mangroves—in your area, consider working them at high tide for snook that have followed bait fish up from the deep holes, basins, and passes bordering the flats. Make longer casts if the water is clear and don't forget their superior eyesight.

Fish for snook at night by rigging lights in your boat or by fishing around bridges where the lights attract bait fish. There is a lot to be said for catching a linesider at night; its head-shaking antics and flared gills go nicely with the silver sheen of its sides in the darkness.

Now it is time for the spotted seatrout.

Spotted Seatrout

Captain Brian Horsley
Flat Out Flyfishing Charters
Outer Banks, North Carolina

Captain Bill Harris
Atlantic Beach, North Carolina

Captain Rodney Smith
Satellite Beach, Florida

Captain Richard Stuhr
Charleston, South Carolina

Captain Bramblett Bradham
Bluffton, South Carolina

THE SPOTTED SEATROUT HAS LEGIONS OF FOLLOWERS. AN ATTRACTIVE FISH WITH clear black spots adorning its silver sides and attention-getting recurvate canine fangs situated right where the action is in the upper jaw, it is found from the mid-Atlantic to the Gulf Coast. The best fly-fishing is found from South Carolina to Texas. North Carolina has the potential for fabulous seatrout action, but its state government allows commercial fishermen— under the direction of the most powerful such lobby in existence, the North Carolina Fisheries Association—to have what conservationists consider free reign to decimate seatrout (and many other) stocks. The only reason North Carolina fly-fishers find any trout at all is because of clever guides like Capt. Brian Horsley and Capt. Bill Harris. They manage to locate trout but can only yearn to see the "gator" trout that is commonplace in the more enlightened Southern states that see the marine environment as something to cherish and protect rather than to rape and plunder.

SEASONS AND SIZES

"Specks," as they are affectionately known, are members of the croaker family that inhabit inshore waters. Their diet consists of shrimp (a favorite), finger mullet, crabs, mummichogs, striped killifish, glass minnows, and various marine invertebrates and mollusks. Average sizes vary considerably depending on many factors, primarily the availability of forage fish and shrimp, the quality of the water and littoral ecosystem, and the ability to reach adulthood. (When Florida reclaimed its waters from inshore commercial fishermen in 1995, it saw a fabulous increase within a year in the number and size of specks being caught.) In Florida, Louisiana, and Texas (states with the most serious seatrout programs, although South Carolina, Georgia, Alabama, and Mississippi are no slouches), at the height of the spring and fall runs, the specks can average 3 pounds, with many larger fish (some weighing nearly 10 pounds) being caught.

In all seatrout states one can catch these fish throughout the year, but the fastest, most consistent action comes in spring and fall. Nevertheless, guides and fly-fishers who can find holding areas in summer and winter have a ball with some fine trout.

Spotted seatrout are excellent fly-fishing targets for three big reasons: 1) Seatrout feed on an array of forage that fly-fishers can mimic with flies; 2) Seatrout inhabit inshore waters that are often easy to access and they feed throughout the water column; and 3) Except in the Tar Heel state, their numbers and sizes appear to be increasing.

TACKLE

Tip- and mid-flex, 8- to 9-foot, 7- to 8-weight fly rods are what I find to be best for seatrout, although Capt. Rodney Smith likes to use a 6-weight because he is deranged. The flies you will be casting aren't especially bulky, and the specks are decent fighters, but not in the same category as bones and drum, so you really don't need any more rod. If you are having trouble on a windy day, use a shooting head.

The reel need not be *spec*tacular (pun intended) with a nauseating price tag. Something akin to a Scientific Anglers System 2 or Ross Gunnison is fine.

Lines need to be diverse to cover all the situations you might find yourself and the specks in. Sometimes the specks are feeding in 2 feet of fairly clear water up against a bank lined with spartina. Sometimes they are in 8 feet of somewhat murky water in moderate current. And sometimes they are sulking in deeper holes with fast current running over them. So, you will need weight-forward, floating, intermediate, sink-tip, and full-sink (often fast) lines.

Leaders should be 8–10 feet long. There is no genuine need to tie your own; just go for one made for you. An 8-pound-test leader is sufficient, but use a 12-inch, 14- to 20-pound shock tippet (the latter is used for true gator trout) made of your favorite abrasion-resistant mono or copolymer to ward off oyster shells, barnacles, and the teeth of the trout.

Specks eat lots of things, so they eat lots of flies that look like those lots of things. (Jeez, you should feel fortunate to be getting such profound advice, eh?)

Rodney throws flies a little more diverse than the traditionals. He likes two creations of his own—the Schroach and Trout Witch (available from Rodney; see the Guides section in the rear of this book)—but he also recommends Dan Blanton's Sar-Mul-Mac, tan and white Clousers, assorted glass minnow imitations, and poppers.

Yes, this monster trout had in fact just eaten a small child who had fallen into the Banana River. Capt. Rodney Smith's client, Rick Hess, saved the day.

Capt. Bill Harris likes Deceivers, Bend-Backs, Clousers, and popping bugs, and ties them in red and white, white, chartreuse, pink and brown, black, green and orange, and chartreuse and red.

Out on the Outer Banks, Capt. Brian Horsely fishes Clousers very heavily. He likes maroon and gold, maroon and brown, gray and white, orange and gold, and green and gold, all with some flash (maybe eight strands) tied in just behind the head of the fly and running all the way back.

Capt. Bramblett Bradham and Capt. Richard Stuhr do cast Deceivers and Clousers, but Bramblett's Swimming Shrimp, which he showed me how to tie in the Orvis shop in Charleston, beats them both. This fly is frighteningly effective on specks.

TACTICS

Spotted seatrout are both roamers and ambushers; they will cruise productive waters or hold tight in deep holes if that's what they feel like at the moment. The key is to determine exactly what they are doing when you are looking for them. To do this you must understand the trout's needs.

Capt. Bramblett Bradham with a dark speck taken from a creek a few hundred yards from Capt. Richard Stuhr's home.

"You should fish the shallow water during the morning and evening, and the deeper shady spots during the heat of the day come late spring and summer," Rodney points out. "Winter-time trout will move in and out of protected water depending on water temps and cold and warm spells. A quiet approach to fishing for trout is always necessary because the larger fish are noise shy."

Rodney, who spends a lot of time on the Indian and Banana Rivers, advises: "Late spring to early fall, you'll find trout on the grass flats, along the mangrove banks, under docks and boats, and on any structure providing shade from the sun. Come winter, trout seek refuge during cold spells in warm-water haunts and places where they are protected from a cold north or northwest wind. Trout prefer canals with a mud bottom that absorbs the sun's heat; the mud releases the heat at night, keeping the trout warm. Also, deep-water canals, creeks, and rivers that connect to the lagoon (the famed Banana River Lagoon and Indian River Lagoon) provide warmer water and protection from the wind."

If all else fails, I suggest hitting the shady water beneath docks and elevated boat houses. The last time I was in Florida, I had good results by getting flies beside or right up under docks and boathouses in the Cocoa Beach area.

Bill does a lot of creek and river fishing, and he casts flies near rock jetties like those at Fort Macon and Cape Lookout. Small bait fish gather in such spots, and Bill exploits the situation with a level of expertise few can equal. And, like Rodney, Bill hits the dark mud deep holes, especially during fall and winter, and if that hole has a mud flat beside it (with shallow water that will warm up in the afternoon and attract bait fish), all the better.

Brian seems to really like the grass flats of the Outer Banks. Clousers cast out over the flats are the most productive, but he will also hit the surf and inlets if that's where he thinks the trout are. His estimates as to the specks' whereabouts aren't often wrong.

Richard and Bramblett are creek specialists, and with so many creeks available in the Charleston area, it's no wonder. Richard and his lovely wife, Mary, live on one of those fer-

If you can't get at the specks, you can't catch them. Flat-bottomed boats like this one owned by Florida's Capt. Jim Hammond (that's renowned outdoor photographer Darrell Jones on the left) are excellent for getting back up the sloughs and over the flats on thin water.

tile creeks, where we have caught many trout within casting distance of their dock. Both guides look for spits and points where water is running around the tip. They'll get down current from the point and cast flies into the eddy and edges. Short, quick strips with Deceivers, Clousers, and of course Bramblett's Swimming Shrimp, are usually on the mark.

Before we move along, I feel obliged to warn you that these fish can cause great passion and poor judgment in anglers. One autumn morning, while fishing with George Misko at the swing bridge over the Atlantic

Fly-fishing writer Jon Cave works a fly on a Florida slough.

Intracoastal Waterway behind North Carolina's Onslow Beach, I was forced to chase another angler from the water with serious promises of bodily harm.

George and I were in the water at about 4 A.M., long before the sun came up. It was cold, and we had every reason to expect a repeat of the previous day's action, which garnered us about a dozen trout. No one else was there, and the water and bank offered hundreds of yards for the anglers we knew would be showing up shortly.

A few minutes after we began casting, here comes another angler, which made three including George and me. George and I were about 25 feet apart, and this bozo steps right in between us.

George began laughing in that demented, knowing laugh of his (he is a former Marine interrogator). It started.

"Hey [here I used a colorful description of a body part], do you think you can get any closer? I mean, why don't you just climb right inside my waders?" I asked pleasantly.

George left the water and was thrashing about on the bank, apparently having some sort of a seizure and making weird noises while trying to catch his breath.

"I was fishing here yesterday," came the clever reply from the rude interloper. Yes, he was asserting that because he had fished in this spot the day before, he had rights to it today.

I anointed the fellow with several more graphic, yet quaint, colloquialisms and started toward him, my rod waving menacingly about and the distance between us rapidly falling away.

Well, he fled the scene and that was that. As I indicated, specks can make you crazy.

OK, let's run offshore for some king mackerel.

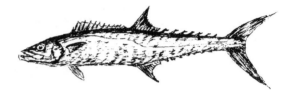

Captain Bill Harris
Atlantic Beach, North Carolina

Captain Lee Manning
Nancy Lee Sportfishing Charters
Swansboro, North Carolina

SOME KING MACKEREL ARE "MONEY" FISH. THAT IS, FROM TEXAS TO VIRGINIA, "BIG money" tournaments draw hundreds, maybe thousands of contestants who try to catch a "money" fish, which is a king that wins them some cash, perhaps several tens of thousands of dollars in cash, actually. I used to fish in these tournaments in North Carolina, but I haven't seen any advertised since I moved to Colorado; kings are pretty scarce here, I suppose (well, at least I haven't caught any).

Actually, I stopped fishing in tournaments because: 1) I never won any money; and 2) I became highly suspicious, as are many, *many* other anglers, when I kept seeing the same professional anglers, all sponsored by big-name boat manufacturers, always winning and placing and racing away from the check-in tent at warp speed in their fabulous boats after dropping off their "money" fish. I mean, do the same five or six B.A.S.S. pros win nearly every time in every B.A.S.S. tournament? Of course not: The odds are stacked against them because plenty of other expert anglers are fishing right beside them. But king mackerel tournaments are different in more ways than one.

I was told by one former professional angler that the same guys always win because the fish they weigh in weren't caught anywhere near the tournament waters. For instance, he says he knows one North Carolina team wins so often because they hire a plane to hustle down to Florida and buy the biggest, freshest king to be found, then to hurry back to a spot located by GPS (Global Positioning System) about 50 miles off the coast of North Carolina and drop the fish in an air-tight container beside the waiting contestants' boat. (They are in radio contact and have radar on the boat to tell them if any other boats are around.)

Sounds pretty far-fetched, eh?

Well, when the winnings are enough to buy a house, you can see why some disgruntled anglers—like me—start to wonder. The way I figure it, if I am not winning the tournament, then someone is cheating better than me, and I won't tolerate that.

But hey, maybe those guys really are just the best.

Working the structure really pays off.

Anyway, those same tournaments don't allow fly-fishing for the kings. Why? Because a knowledgeable fly-fisher can frequently come up with bigger kings than the guys slow-trolling live bait or hauling a ribbonfish on a down-rigger. There is no other reason whatsoever for not allowing fly tackle to be used.

This is good news for fly-fishers.

Kings, which are fish of both green and blue water, frequently are caught from just outside the surf (even from piers) to many miles offshore, and they come right inside inlets, too. I have seen a lot of nice kings caught well inside Beaufort Inlet between Morehead City and Atlantic Beach, North Carolina. They feed on an array of bait fish, including Spanish and scaled sardines, menhaden, snappers, pinfish, grunts, ribbonfish, thread herring, flying fish, bluefish, spotted seatrout, gray trout, and mullet, among many other species. You can see by that menu that kings range throughout the water column and from inshore to far offshore.

More a subtropical and tropical species, kings prefer water temperatures from the high 60s to the high 80s. They are caught along the mid-Atlantic coast perhaps as far north as southern New England, but I disagree with three references that claim kings are caught off the Maine coast. I have never heard of such a thing and seriously doubt it, although I suppose *anything's* possible. My rationale is that kings do not like water below 68 degrees, and Maine gets the icy Labrador current, not the warm Gulf Stream. I suspect Massachusetts is their northernmost hunting ground.

Kings are structure-oriented fish, and that structure might take the form of deep current upwellings, flotsam, sargassum, current convergence, shoals and reefs, rocks, wrecks, buoys, and any other anomaly that attracts bait fish. They are also pretty voracious, and it is their appetite and their fondness for structure that the fly-fisher exploits.

SEASONS AND SIZES

King seasons are dictated by water temperature and forage availability, as well as by salinity: They prefer water with 32–36 parts salt per thousand, although they do inhabit water with higher and lower counts. So, if the water in your stretch of the western Atlantic or Gulf of Mexico is about 79 degrees, has 34 parts salt per thousand, and has good numbers of the edibles kings are known to enjoy, then you are probably in luck. The thing is, however, that you have to catch them, and sometimes that can be frustrating.

Kings get mighty big, folks. The average size, like the bluefish, depends on the school you hit and the region's proclivity toward holding big kings, plus that ever-present luck. They weigh up to 90 pounds, but the biggest taken on the fly weighed 55

An average king from North Carolina.

"Smokers" like this will kill a discount reel.

pounds; it was caught off Key West, where many records are set for kings on the fly. However, if I had to say what the average king taken on the fly weighs, I would estimate about 10 pounds. Still, plenty of bigger fish are caught all the time.

TACKLE

The rod can start at about a 9-weight and go to a 12-weight for areas with abundant large kings. The rod needs to be powerful enough to throw a streamer or other heavy fly in the wind, and it has to have the backbone to put the skids to the fish when it runs toward a buoy or other structure that can break you off. Tip-flex rods at least 9 feet long are needed. My standard king rod is a 9-foot-long 9-weight.

The reel must have a solid drag and enough line capacity to hold not only the line, but also 250 yards of 30-pound Dacron backing. Kings will smoke a cheesy reel. In fact, big kings are called *smokers* for the way they can burn line and drags.

Lines are usually intermediate weight-forwards, but from time to time a fast sink-tip or full-sink comes in handy. Shooting heads are very nice to have on windy days or when throwing really big flies, or both.

Stu Apte's Tarpon Fly is a natural for kings, too.

Leaders have got to be tough. Use a 10-foot, 20-pound class leader with a 12-inch, 50-pound shock tippet—or better yet, a 30-pound, braided wire bite guard. Kings have serious teeth.

Now the flies. Jeez, I have used a lot of different types and caught fish with many of them. 2/0 to 4/0 Deceivers, bunker patterns, and squid patterns are all worth a try. The colors can really vary. Experiment. If I had to pick a color combination to start off cold, I would go with dark green over gray, and it would be a Deceiver (created by Lefty Kreh, one of the greats). Other very good patterns include the Big-Eyed Baitfish, Lou Tabory's Slab Fly and Sea Rat, Stu Apte's Tarpon Fly, and Curcione's Sardina.

TACTICS

Capt. Lee Manning has been fishing out of Bogue Inlet at Swansboro, North Carolina, for 30 years. With that kind of experience, you might expect him to have some concrete ideas about finding and catching kings. He does.

The answer to the riddle of finding kings consistently, according to Lee, is knowing where the structure is (that's the easy part) and how to work it. You see, anyone can find structure, but comparatively few know how to work it. Lee knows how.

Capt. Lee Manning with a brace of Bogue Inlet kings.

"The key is to keep whatever you are using over the structure as long as possible. If the kings are there and they feel like eating, they will eat, but they have to see what you've got," says one of North Carolina's most experienced charter captains.

Lee fishes a bit differently than the other guys. He does not feel the need to run 35 miles offshore first thing in the morning. Instead, he starts right outside Bogue Inlet and begins by working 20, maybe 30 feet down to find kings cruising at that level in a more comfortable layer of water, waiting for the sun to warm the surface water. Once it warms up, the kings often come up.

And when Lee gets focused on a piece of structure, he will stay on it until he is very sure that either no kings are on it, or they have lockjaw. I have seen him work the Keypost (a piece of structure) outside of Bogue Inlet back and forth for an hour, covering what seemed like every cubic yard of water until what may have been the only king there couldn't stand it anymore. And I have seen him work the water around a buoy by slowly circling it time and again until a fish hooked up.

Capt. Bill Harris believes in chumming the kings right up to the boat. He will catch buckets of menhaden and finger mullet, then put some of the fish through a meat grinder. This he ladles into the water while tossing chunks and the occasional live bait fish into the water to get the kings interested. When he sees one come into the slick, he opens fire with a well-placed cast. From his custom-built Jones Brothers Cape Fisherman, this process becomes a science. Bill's enthusiasm and cutting-edge fly-fishing philosophy bring nationally recognized fly-fishers to his boat.

No matter how you work the structure, always record its location in your GPS or Loran C. Keep a logbook of water temperatures, surface conditions, sunlight, currents, bait fish seen or recorded on your graph, sizes of fish and the depths they hit at, and any other factor you feel may be relevant. Get to know other anglers and get structure fixes from them, too, and share yours.

When you hook a king, you can expect it to run and run fast. It might make several runs during the course of a fight, and it might jump 10 feet out of the water. Be ready for these jumps and bow to the fish when it does so.

Now let's talk about one of the most underfished inshore fighters, the little tunny, a.k.a. false albacore.

Little Tunny

23

Captain Bill Harris
Atlantic Beach, North Carolina

Tom Earnhardt
Author of *Fly Fishing the Tidewaters*
Raleigh, North Carolina

THE LITTLE TUNNY, ALSO KNOWN AS FALSE ALBACORE, MAY BE THE MOST UNDER-fished game fish along the eastern seaboard. I am not sure why. Perhaps it is because the "fat Albert" isn't highly regarded as food fare, but that, in my opinion, is a poor reason for a lack of respect. The little tunny has plenty of attributes that more than make up for it not being a very good meal for humans.

I caught my first little tunny about half a mile outside of North Carolina's Bogue Inlet. A school swam by Fred Kluge and me as we were heading back in Fred's Grady-White, and we hit one fish. That little tunny—and it was little, weighing perhaps 8 pounds—was like dynamite: For such a small package, it packed one hell of a wallop. I have loved them ever since.

But not all little tunny are that small.

SEASONS AND SIZES

These compact members of the tuna family can weigh up to 35 pounds, although the largest recorded on the fly weighed just more than 19 pounds, it being caught off the Dry Tortugas (near Key West). I suspect they probably average 10–15 pounds or so. Like the king mackerel and bluefish, this game fish shows up en masse at different times of the year in different places, but in some areas you can find them throughout the year. In North Carolina, for instance, the major run occurs in the fall, with October and November being prime months and the fish still hanging around often well into December. But then again, you could catch one in May. They are known for popping up when you least expect them.

TACKLE

Little tunny are strong fish, as are all tuna that live in both inshore and offshore waters. (I have caught them 20 miles offshore and within casting distance of the beach.)

North Carolina's Cape Lookout is often an excellent spot to try false albacore on the fly, especially in a Jones Brothers Cape Fisherman.

Wind conditions can be demanding, meaning you need powerful rods to throw flies accurately. A high-modulus, 9- to 11-weight rod at least 9 feet long will also allow you to—if you know how and if you dare—put great pressure on the tunny to turn it and wear it out as quickly as possible. The faster the fish is brought to the boat, the better the chances it will survive release, which is exactly what you want to do with most little tunny.

The reel must—*must*—be an excellent piece of equipment fully capable of handling long, repeated, screaming runs of 100 yards or more. Got a *fairly* reliable drag? It won't do. And the reel must hold at least 250 yards of 30-pound Dacron backing, to be safe.

Fly lines are easy. Floating or intermediate weight-forward lines are all that is required.

Leaders have to be able to take the teeth of the little tunny and also be heavy enough at the butt to cast the fly correctly. Capt. Bill Harris suggests a 30- to 40-pound, 4-foot butt section with a 4-foot, 12- to 16-pound tippet.

Like Bill, I have found that two fly patterns are all you need to catch little tunny: Lefty's Deceiver and the Clouser Minnow, about 1 to 1/0. Chartreuse, gray and white, and green and white are often too tempting for the tunny to pass up. Author Tom Earnhardt adds Bob Popovic's Surf Candy to that short list.

TACTICS

The most fanatical little tunny angler I know is Tom Earnhardt. The dean of Tar Heel saltwater fly-fishers, Tom hunts them with a passion and has it down to a science. And Tom has a way of finding these fish in places most other anglers don't even realize hold a great fighting fish.

"I know of several places where they can be caught with regularity in waist-deep water during October and November," says the ayatollah of albacore.

Frankly, you might hit a pod of false albacore anywhere, from miles out to sea right on the surface, to near points and inlets, and even within a double haul of the beach. But like all game fish, they pattern themselves according to their needs.

Efficient predators constantly on the move, little tunny are always in search of prey to sustain their high metabolism. Find the food under favored conditions, and you will often find the tunny.

Bill and Tom say that early in the fall along the North Carolina coast, little tunny can be found along shoals and points. But as autumn progresses, more bait fish are swept along inlets, and the tunny follow. This means thousands of tunny may be where there were none a month earlier.

Hit the inlets in the late fall, especially deep water inlets like Bogue and Beaufort. Also in the late fall you can find huge numbers of bait fish right in the

The dean of North Carolina saltwater fly-fishers, Tom Earnhardt, with a colorful little tunny.

Nancy Lee Fishing Charters mate Jeff Warren and Rocky the fish-fetching Labrador show off another nice little tunny.

surf, so working the beaches can be very rewarding.

Watch for birds. Little tunny are one of the surest of all the game fish along the mid-Atlantic coast that can be marked by birds diving in the water to attack the bait fish the tunny are feeding on.

Bill is particularly keen on the angler's ability to cast quickly and accurately. Sometimes a school of tunny will only appear on the surface to feed for a few seconds, attacking a shoal of bait fish that scatters quickly and sends the tunny back down to wait for another opportunity. You need to get a lot of line out and put the fly in the water near the feeding tunny.

"Albacore fishing is fast and furious, but can be frustrating due to fish showing up for small periods of time during the day," as Bill says. "Fishermen may have one chance or 50 chances to catch fish based on water temperature and amounts of fish."

Offshore, I have found binoculars beneficial for spotting passing tunny, especially on calm days when the school can be seen quite a ways off, even without birds. Sometimes the school is just moving from place to place and not feeding, and the birds know this. However, tunny will often readily strike a fly that they see near the school, even if they are not "feeding" at that time.

Care for some crevalle jack?

Crevalle Jack

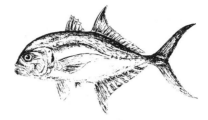

24

Captain Bramblett Bradham
Bluffton, South Carolina

Captain Richard Stuhr
Charleston, South Carolina

A FEW YEARS AGO I WAS TRYING TO GET ANY FISH'S ATTENTION DOWN IN PORT Canaveral, without much luck. Suddenly my rod bent with a surprisingly hard take and I was sure I had finally succeeded in tricking a speck (spotted seatrout) or drum. Within a few seconds, however, the yellowish flash in the water near the sea wall told me that my prize was neither: I had fooled a very young crevalle jack, often just called a "jack" or a "jack crevalle." The precocious little bugger was no more than 10 inches long, if that, and I marveled at how hard these fish can hit. I tossed him back in.

Capt. Richard Stuhr works a school of Charleston Harbor jacks as the author's wife, Susan, critiques his casting technique.

A year later I found myself in a flats boat with Capt. Bramblett Bradham, dead smack in the middle of beautiful, historic Charleston Harbor. Capt. Richard Stuhr was 100 yards from us in his ActionCraft flats boat with my wife Susan standing on the bow platform with a long-lens camera.

Appearing as radiant scythes slowly slicing their way toward Fort Sumter, three dozen shining, golden tails were illuminated by the soft rays of the morning sun as they cut the calm surface.

"Bob! Bob!" exclaimed my genial guide in a soft but obviously excited voice behind me. "Jacks! Big ones!" But my eyes were already on the approaching school.

"I see them," I replied in a hushed but equally excited tone.

"Put the fly right in front of them and strip it fast straight away. Cast now."

I put the 9-weight rod into action with a set of powered-up double hauls and sent the big popper to a point 6 feet ahead of the school. I began to strip as fast as I could and made as much noise with the popper as possible.

"Here he comes," Bramblett announced, not even trying to conceal his excitement. "He's going to eat it!"

The enormous jack at the head of the school rushed forward and engulfed the fly in a long, smooth gulp.

"Hit him! Hit him!" Bramblett yelled, no longer hushed.

I struck hard to the side and then struck a second time, feeling the hook sink deep and well. The school scattered but my rod bent under the boat right to the reel, the jack screaming down and away and the line disappearing from the sturdy Odyssey reel at an alarming rate.

"Get around the trolling motor," Bramblett commanded, but I was already moving that way and somehow managed to keep the line—make that the backing by this point—out of the prop. Now I could maneuver.

The long green rod shuddered in my hands as the great fish raced away from the boat.

And then it was gone. The rod straightened up and I was left with the sickening feeling of losing a colossal fish.

"What happened," a despondent Bramblett asked with a mortified look on his face.

"I dunno." I quickly reeled in and grabbed the leader, the fly long gone. "Bit me off clean," I said flatly, looking at the failed leader.

"What pound test tippet do you have on?"

"Sixteen, man."

"Oh, damn, Bob. You gotta have a lot heavier tippet than that. A lot heavier."

And thus began my education in the science of catching trophy crevalle jacks on the fly.

I am still learning.

SEASONS AND SIZES

Crevalle jacks are not often hotly pursued by fly-fishers. Most are caught in Florida waters and the Gulf of Mexico incidentally by anglers after snook, red drum, and seatrout. I must admit that I have no idea why, as the jack is a beautiful fish and a strong fighter that can grow to more than 50 pounds, although a fish half that size is considered good by anyone's standards. Me? Any time I see or suspect jacks in an area, I seek them out.

Although very common in Florida waters, I believe the largest schools of trophy jacks are to be found in Charleston Harbor during the summer, from May to mid-August. Oddly, surprisingly few cast flies there for these behemoths. Perhaps this chapter will put a few more fly-fishers onto these beauties. Bramblett and Richard know the fish average 20–30 pounds, with what Bramblett says are "many world records swimming around" (34 pounds and up; in my opinion I feel the most susceptible category is the 20-pound line class, which as of this writing is only a 34-pound jack). Having seen these fish milling around there, I can confirm Bramblett's claim.

TACKLE

Well, you have already learned the importance of tackle, so let's talk about the rest of the gear you'll need.

Rods should be about 9 feet long, and 9- to 12-weight with a 10-weight being just about right. Yes, you need rods this long and heavy because of the size and strength of the jacks, and the size of the poppers and streamers you will be casting to them.

Your reel must have a reliable drag—you'll need it—and a large capacity. Jacks make long, fast, repeated runs that will have the line fleeing the reel like when fighting bonefish and permit, only jacks are much larger. Skimp on a reel here and you will be disappointed.

Jacks are right on top, so you will be sight-casting to them with a floating weight-forward or a floating line with a shooting head. You won't need your sink-tips, intermediates, or full-sinks in Charleston Harbor.

Ahem, leaders and tippets. Okay, 16-pound tippets are out unless you are hunting for an IGFA record. Your shock tippet should be—pay attention—50- to 80-pound test, about 12–18 inches worth (a max of 12 inches for IGFA rules). Tie this to a 20-pound class leader 8–10 feet long. Yes, I was just a bit light.

Big jacks demand big, tasty-looking, exciting flies. Richard and Bramblett use large red and white, white with glitter, and yellow poppers, equally large yellow Deceivers with gold Mylar piping, and what Bramblett admits are "giant white or yellow Clousers." Richard also recommends large Whistlers, Sea-Ducers, and bunker flies.

TACTICS

Tactics for Charleston's man-eating crevalle jacks are fairly simple and straightforward. Watch Richard and Bramblett and you get the idea quickly.

Do not go blasting out into the middle of Charleston Harbor, skid to a stop, and then start looking for fish up top. No. You start looking while well away from the harbor with the motor off. Use binoculars to scan the water. You are looking for "nervous" water and often the tails of the jacks themselves. These fish won't be feeding like a school of marauding blues, mind you. They will be quietly milling about and are very skittish.

Once you spot them, use the trolling motor to get into position in front of them. Do not get too close because if they hear the outboard they will vanish and pop up somewhere away from you and that motor. See where they are heading, move ahead of them to an intercept position, and hope they don't change direction on you (which they do with annoying regularity).

Now get the fly out there. Make as long a cast as possible, for fish you see coming a ways off (although sometimes the jacks suddenly appear close to a boat with quiet fly-

Believe it or not, this is a typical Charleston Harbor jack. Yes, you really should call your travel agent and Bramblett and Richard today.

The right action on the fly means jacks like this.

fishers). Richard says you need to make quick, accurate 60- to 80-foot casts with this tackle.

Forget twitching the popper or streamer. Impart as much action onto the fly as you can with vigorous jerks of the rod tip and powerful strips. Jacks are predators used to bait fish fleeing in abject terror, so make your fly do a nice, frantic dance as though convinced that if it didn't escape there would be no tomorrow.

Be calm when the jack rushes forward to eat your fly. Yes, this is easier said than done, but you must avoid striking too soon. When you feel a bit of tension and weight from the fish, hit him hard with a full waist twist, just as you would a tarpon. Now hang on!

This is going to take a while. The fight, that is. Keep pressure on the fish and try to anticipate its runs, which are deliberate and impressive. Don't attempt to net or gaff the fish until it is tired enough to be handled, but not so exhausted that it won't survive release due to of the tremendous build up of lactic acid in its tissue. (That's why you need to keep the pressure on the fish and wear it down as fast as you can.)

Listen, it's hot out there come summer. Drink plenty of water, bring sunblock and rain gear (thunderstorms, you know), wear a brimmed hat, and wear polarized sunglasses.

And call Bramblett and Richard! (Like all the guides listed in this book, their numbers are in the Guides section.) A great second choice is the Banana River Lagoon's bridge abutments. Call Capt. Rodney Smith.

25 Fly-Fishing and the Conservationist

GO UP TO ANY FISHING GUIDE OR LONG-TIME ANGLER, AND THAT PERSON WILL tell you that the fishing isn't what it used to be. There are fewer fish caught today than 20 years ago, and the fish caught are often smaller. You will also discover that many species of fish, both baitfish and gamefish, have disappeared or have become endangered. And if you look around, you'll see that it isn't just the fisheries, but our whole environment that has changed. What has been the cause of this drastically reduced quality in fishing?

Southern California once enjoyed one of the most prolific near-shore fisheries imaginable. The Golden State's kelp beds, which lie just offshore in view of the beaches, fostered a myriad of game fish, ranging from yellowtail, calico bass, white seabass, California barracuda, and California sheephead, to lingcod, spotted kelp bass, mackerel, and halibut. California's surf was known as a fabulous place to catch a variety of colorful surf perch and the feisty California corbina. Today, with unchecked growth and antiquated pollution control technologies, these fish populations have been drastically reduced.

Along the West Coast, various species of salmon are in dire straits. Hydroelectric dams have blocked access to traditional salmon spawning grounds; water quality degradation has further dimmed their plight. Governments have tried to respond, but they often fall short. The California State Fish and Game Commission grudgingly gave one species, the spring-run Chinook, "monitored species" status, though "endangered" status may have been more appropriate for this fish; its population has dropped from one million to about ten thousand in recent memory.

The East Coast is not without similar problems. One would think that hog farming would have little effect upon fisheries, but in North Carolina, where sprawling corporate hog farms abound, creeks, streams, and rivers continually suffer from the leaching of hog waste lagoons. And these lagoons do rupture—an all-too-common occurrence in North Carolina. Sometimes tens of millions of gallons of untreated hog waste rush into the waterways and begin to make their way downstream to the sea. Along the way, innumerable fish die and float to the surface, forming vast mats of dead game fish and bait fish.

Additionally, the quality of our waters has suffered from poor timber practices. When an area is clear-cut the runoff causes streams to silt, and the lack of shade raises water temperature. This kills off or seriously impairs game fish populations. Adding to the problem are U.S. Forest Service officials "in bed" with timber giants like Boise Cascade, who see the national forests as their own personal bank accounts.

Government agencies and large corporations are not the only ones responsible for the plight of our waters and the fish populations. According to the Environmental Protection Agency, nonpoint pollution sources, which are sources spread out over large areas (agricultural and urban runoff, for instance, as opposed to point sources like factories and mills), are responsible for about 60 percent of our water pollution. Nonpoint pollution sources include you and me. Individually, we have little impact, but when you take 100 million people, and each person throws a small piece of trash on the ground, drains the car oil on the roadside, or fertilizes the lawn, well, it all adds up.

It should become apparent from these few instances that our presence on this land and our desire for progress, or even just to feed ourselves, affects the environment around us, more often than not to its detriment. What are we to do? Conserve. Conservation is the key to sustaining healthy waters (and our environment) in North America. More often than not, conservation manifests itself in government acts. And if not for the Clean Water Act, the situation would be a lot worse.

THE CLEAN WATER ACT

In 1972, a furious American public, physically and spiritually sick from the grievous damage done to their waters by chemical manufacturers, automobile plants, steel mills, pulp mills, and seemingly countless other sources, saw Congress pass one of the most sweeping and effective environmental protection measures ever conceived: The Federal Water Pollution Control Act, better known as the Clean Water Act. This Act proved to be the most important and beneficial achievement in the history of American environmentalism and conservationism.

Since the Act was signed into law by President Nixon, billions of pounds of industrial pollutants have been banished from our water. The number of sewage treatment plants that provide secondary or higher waste treatment (secondary treatment eliminates at least 85 percent of the waste) is approaching 100 percent. The level of contaminants in our water from nonpoint sources has dropped markedly. And untold millions of dollars in fines have been levied against polluters who see no reason to abide by this act.

Nevertheless, we still have a lot of work to do.

THE FISHING INDUSTRY

Though the polluting of our waters has had a critical effect on the fish populations, it is not the only cause of reduced fish populations. Overfishing by the commercial fishing industry has also had a significant effect. The Magnuson Fishery Conservation and Management Act has attempted to protect and nurture U.S. fish populations, assuring enough fish for commercial and recreational anglers.

Until 1976, foreign fishing fleets were able to legally fish the territorial waters of the United States. As important fish stocks plummeted to alarmingly low numbers, which in turned affected U.S. coastal economies, Congress stepped in and created the Magnuson Fishery Act. This act gave the U.S. government "sole authority" over the fish living within 200 miles of our shores. Without foreign competition, U.S. fisherman would have more

Commercial fishing boats at a North Carolina dock. North Carolina is the only coastal state with a commercial fishing industry that is still allowed to ravage these shoreline areas.

Florida's Indian River Lagoon is again teeming with fish and may again become a genuine angler's paradise.

fish to catch. Knowing that the problem would emerge again if commercial fisheries growth remained unchecked, the Magnuson Act attempted to regulate the commercial fishing industry by setting catch limits. The intent was to maintain a viable fish population and prevent particular species from being fished out.

Unfortunately, the act backfired; it failed to clearly define the meaning of "overfishing." As a result, the industry has defined overfishing itself by using market and social values rather than fisheries science. The act itself compounded the problem by calling for the government to work toward "optimum yield" for the commercial fishing industry. This puts the emphasis on more of an economic than a conservationist footing. Therefore even if a particular fish population has been overfished, if the economics of the situation demands continued harvesting, then fishing will continue. The result: the near total collapse of our commercial fisheries. Rather than nurturing and sustaining the commercial fishing industry, tens of thousands of jobs in the commercial fishing industry have been lost since 1976, and billions and billions of dollars in revenues went with them. This also means reduced fish populations and a lesser quality in recreational angling.

Governmental acts aren't always disastrous. In Florida, shore-netting practices had drastically decreased important game fish—which is bad for recreational and commercial fishers alike. On July 1, 1995, the Save Our

Sealife (SOS) constitutional amendment went into effect and effectively banned inshore netting in the Sunshine State. In just two years, remarkable increases have been noted in the average size and number of game fish, including spotted seatrout, red drum, ladyfish, flounder, snook, and crevalle jack, as well as many other species.

This amendment has seen legal challenges by the netters, but so far these challenges have been turned away in the courts. Since the Florida amendment took effect, other coastal states have noted the program's tremendous success, and many are working on or have already passed similar amendments.

WHAT CAN FLY-FISHERS DO?

One thing fly-fishers can do is practice a catch-and-release philosophy wherever they are. This philosophy was founded by A. J. McClane and Lee Wulff, two angling legends now passed on. They are owed a great debt by us all for championing the idea that a fish is too valuable to catch only once. And there is much scientific evidence that, when done right, catch-and-release techniques allow most released fish to survive with no ill effects. This is not to say that keeping a legal fish every now and then to enjoy at the dinner table is wrong.

Another possibility is to join an environmental organization and work to protect fisheries at a grassroots level. The combined resources of pro-fishing organizations form impressive force with the ability to influence public opinion. The Federation of Fly Fishers, National Audubon Society, Coastal Conservation Association, Ducks Unlimited (North America's leading wetlands protection organization), and Trout Unlimited, as well as highly responsible corporate entities like The Orvis Company, Sage, and L.L. Bean, are leading the fight in fisheries resource conservation. They deserve your lifelong support.

Conservation issues have often evolved into battlegrounds between two opposing forces—commercial fishers on one side, recreational fishers on the other. One side sees a threat to their livelihood, the other to their ability to enjoy the outdoors. The question is, will we continue to battle each other, or will we work together to create a sustainable fish population that will benefit both parties? If we ever intend to truly save our vanishing resources for our children, and our children's children, we must join forces.

It is up to fly-fishermen and conservationists of the nation to put a stop to the people, organizations, and practices that have mismanaged our waters and fisheries for far too long. We are stewards of the environment, and our actions must begin to reflect our words, lest the ruin of our environment continue unchecked. We must all lend our voices, deeds, and checkbooks to this end.

part

5

APPENDIXES

Guides, Lodges, and Contributing Fly-Fishers

Chuck Ash
Brightwater Alaska, Inc.
PO Box 110796
Anchorage, AK 99511
Phone: (907) 344-1340
Fax: (907) 344-4614
Chuck is a remarkably savvy salmon and char angler with decades of guiding experience in the Bristol Bay watershed. If you are going to Alaska, see him first.

Capt. Bramblett Bradham
13C Edgewater Circle
Bluffton, SC 29910
Phone: (803) 837-2044
Having caught many fish with Bramblett, I can personally assure you that he is a very motivated and crafty guide. Fly-fishers come from everywhere to learn from Bramblett and fish with him. Bramblett is an Orvis-endorsed guide.

Capt. Harold Carlin
Fin Quest
Hatteras, NC 27943
Phone: (919) 995-5060
Harold is a noted red drum expert who finds and catches some of the biggest reds on the planet.

Capt. Bob Dove
PO Box 414
Islamorada, FL 33036
Phone: (800) 262-9112
Bob's exploits in the Florida backcountry, Florida Bay, and the Islamorada region of the Keys are almost legendary.

Tom Earnhardt
Raleigh, NC
Tom wrote the acclaimed Fly Fishing the Tidewaters *and is one of the most respected saltwater fly-fishers in the Southeast.*

Brian and Sharon Elder
Wollaston Lake Lodge
6000 Douglas Drive North
Minneapolis, MN 55429-2314
Phone: (800) 328-0628
Mpls.: (612) 533-7752
(September-May)
Lodge: (306) 633-2032 (June-August)
Fax: (612) 533-9156 (September-May)
Wollaston Lake Lodge offers the best giant northern pike fly-fishing in Saskatchewan.

Mickey and Maggie Greenwood
Blackfire Flyfishing Guest Ranch
PO Box 981
Angel Fire, New Mexico 87710
Phone: (505) 377-6870
Fax: (505) 377-3807
*Mickey and Maggie run a unique
lodge high in the Sangre de Cristo
Mountains. The rainbows and cutts
are gorgeous, plentiful, and large.
One of the best trout experiences I
have ever had.*

Andre Godin
Auberge Miramichi Inn
PO Box 331
Red Bank, New Brunswick
Canada E9E 2P3
Phone: (506) 836-7452
*Andre directs the catching of more
Atlantic salmon than anyone else I
know.*

Capt. Bill Harris
2721 University Drive
Durham, NC 27707
Phone: (919) 808-2936
*From his fishing headquarters in
Atlantic Beach, Bill continues to be
on the cutting edge of North Carolina
saltwater fly-fishing. He is extremely
knowledgeable and personable and a
good friend.*

Capt. Les Hill
265-B Lomond Drive
Port Charlotte, FL 33953
Phone: (914) 743-6622
*Les is one of the better-known guides
for snook, drum, tarpon, trout, and
other inshore game fish in the famous
Port Charlotte area.*

Capt. Brian Horsley
PO Box 387
227 S Woodland Drive
Nagshead, NC 27959
Phone: (919) 449-0562
*Brian is the leading fly-fishing
guide on the famous Outer Banks
and a columnist for* The Sportfishing Report. *Need I say more?*

Capt. Mark Houghtaling
15920 SW 85th Avenue
Miami, FL 33157
Phone: (305) 253-1151
*When in Miami, Mark is the man
for dolphin fishing. Miami isn't
often thought of by traveling fly-
fishers as a great destination, but
this is to your advantage.*

Dr. Jay
Dr. Jay's Guide Service
PO Box 99145
Raleigh, NC 27624
Phone: (919) 518-2375
*Dr. Jay's reputation as a producer of
giant bluegill speaks for itself. He
finds them when no one else can.*

Capt. Doug Jowett
61 Four Wheel Drive
Brunswick, ME 04011
Phone: (207) 725-4573
*Doug is an accomplished outdoor
writer and striper guide, one of the
most experienced on the Maine
coast.*

Capt. Pat Keliher
157 Durham Road
Freeport, ME 04032
Phone: (207) 865-6561
Pat, who is Orvis-endorsed, is a popular striper guide on Maine's rocky and beautiful coast.

Al Maas
PO Box 353
200 Summit Avenue
Walker, MN 56484
Phone: (218) 547-1600
Al is a highly sought-after speaker and guide whose complete understanding of the fish of the Minnesota northland is legendary. One of the very best.

Capt. Lee Manning
Nancy Lee Sportfishing Charters
Swansboro, NC 28584
Phone: (919) 354-FISH
Lee is absolutely a top guide on the North Carolina Coast.

Jennifer and Lars Olsson
PO Box 132
Bozeman, MT 59771
Phone: (406) 585-9625
Jennifer and Lars are two leading fly-fishing guides in Montana. For memorable trout angling on world-class waters, these are the two guides you need to see.

Bob Pigott
The Fly Fishing Guide
208344 Highway 101
Port Angeles, WA 98363
Phone: (360) 327-3554
Year-round steelhead action brings people to Bob Pigott for big fish in a beautiful setting on the Olympic Peninsula.

George Poveromo
Parkland, FL
One of the greatest saltwater anglers out there, George knows of what he speaks. Respected for his prowess in finding big game fish and plenty of them, his know-how has earned him his position with Salt Water Sportsman. Probably the most experienced dolphin pro anywhere.

Capt. Rodney Smith
PO Box 373257
Satellite Beach, FL 32937
Phone: (407) 777-2773
Captain "Rod" is one of Florida's most knowledgeable and enthusiastic saltwater guides. Seek him out for red drum, tripletail, snook, tarpon, trout, and other game fish. Rod holds and has produced for his clients IGFA record fish, including red drum and tripletail. Rod is a very good friend and one of the sharpest guides and fly-fishers I know.

Mark Sosin
Boca Raton, FL
Mark Sosin has been one of the world's leading authorities on salt-water game fish for more than 30 years. His words in Salt Water Sportsman *and his books, as well as on his television show,* Mark Sosin's Saltwater Journal, *have put more fly-fishers onto big fish than imaginable. A genuine world-class angler.*

Joe Stefanski
Diana Lake Lodge
PO Box 1053
Kuujjuaq, Quebec J0M 1C0
Phone: (800) 662-6404
Fax: (603) 532-6404
Diana Lake Lodge offers some of the best brookie action anywhere.

Capt. Richard Stuhr
547 Sanders Farm Lane
Charleston, SC 29492
Phone: (803) 881-3179
Richard knows the low country and is highly respected as an outstanding guide around the Charleston region. His understanding of drum, crevalle jack, and trout is remarkable. A superior choice in guides, and Orvis-endorsed, of course.

Steve Tooker
HCR 84, Box 990
Walker, MN 56484
Phone: (800) 874-1999
Steve is a long-time professional angler with a reputation for catching the biggest of the big. A popular speaker on the fishing trade show tour, he can't be beat for muskie, bass, and northern pike.

Appendix A:
Fly Rods

Cortland Line Company
3736 Kellogg Road
PO Box 5588
Cortland, NY 13045
Phone: (607) 756-2851
Web: www.cortlandline.com/cortland

The Diamondback Company
Route 100 South
Stowe, VT 05672
Phone: (800) 626-2970
Fax: (802) 253-4570

Fenwick Outdoor Technologies Group
1900 18th Street
Spirit Lake, IO 51360
Phone: (712) 336-1520
Web: www.fenwickfishing.com

Garrison Formula
3637 Medina Road
Medina, OH 44256
Phone: (800) 701-6248
Fax: (330) 722-4329

G. Loomis
1359 Down River Drive
Woodland, WA 98674
Phone: (800) 662-8818
Fax: (360) 225-7169
Web: www.gloomis.com

Hardy USA
PO Box 3987
Evergreen, CO 80437
Phone: (888) HARDYUSA
Fax: (303) 679-9090
Web: www.hardyusa.com

Lamiglas, Inc.
PO Box U
1400 Atlantic
Woodland, WA 98674
Phone: (360) 225-9436
Fax: (360) 225-5050
Web: www.lamiglas.com

L.L. Bean, Inc.
Casco Street
Freeport, ME 04033
Phone: (800) 221-4221
Fax: (207) 552-3080
Web: www.llbean.com/fish
L.L. Bean remains one of the world's top outfitters and their fly rods are absolutely up to standard, from their lower-end Angler Series to their new SPT.

The Orvis Company, Inc.
Historic Route 7A
Manchester, VT 05254
Phone: (800) 548-9548
Fax: (540) 343-7053
Web: www.orvis.com
*Founded by Charles F. Orvis in 1856,
Orvis is one of the world's most respected fly-fishing companies. Their
rods are world class. Orvis was the
first company to get a rod on the
market that substantially reduced
vibration (the Trident rod), which
increased casting efficiency through
damping technology.*

Penn Fishing Tackle Mfg. Co.
3028 West Hunting Park Avenue
Philadelphia, PA 19132
Phone: (215) 229-9415
Penn rods are excellent.

Redington Fly Rods and Reels
906 South Dixie Highway
Stuart, FL 34994
Phone: (800) 253-2538
Fax: (561) 220-9957
Web: www.redington.com

R.L. Winston Rod Company
500 South Main Street
Twin Bridges, MT 59754
Phone: (406) 684-5674
Fax: (406) 684-5533
Web: www.winstonrods.com

Sage Mfg. Corp.
8500 Northeast Day Road
Bainbridge Island, WA 98110
Phone: (800) 533-3004
Fax: (206) 842-6830
Web: www.sageflyfish.com
*Sage is a leading manufacturer of
high-quality fly rods. I have toured
their shop and been through the
manufacturing process from start to
finish, and can personally attest to
Sage's attention to detail and highest of standards.*

Scott Fly Rod Company
2355 Air Park Way
Montrose, CO 81401
Phone: (970) 249-3180
Fax: (970) 249-4172
Web: www.scottflyrod.com
Classy and expertly made.

Thomas & Thomas
2 Avenue A
Turners Falls, MA 01376
Phone: (413) 863-9727
Web: www.flyfishers.com/
thomas-thomas

3M Scientific Anglers
3M Center
Bldg. 223-4N-05
St. Paul, MN 55144
Phone: (800) 430-5000
Web: www.mmm.com

Versitex of America
3545 Schuylkill Road
Spring City, PA 19475
Phone: (610) 948-4442
Fax: (800) 331-6406

Appendix B:
Fly Reels

Aaron Reels
10141-9 Evening Star Drive
Grass Valley, CA 95945
Phone: (800) 437-3578
Fax: (916) 272-8549

Abel Reels
165 Aviador Street
Camarillo, CA 93010
Phone: (800) 848-7335
Fax: (805) 482-0701
Web: www.abelreels.com\abel
*Although I don't own one, I have
used Abel reels and know several
guides who swear by them. Their
reputation for indestructible drags
is legendary.*

Adams Reels
PO Box 183
Cambridge, NY 12816
Phone: (518) 677-2276

Bauer Premium Fly Reels
401 Corral de Tierra Road
Salinas, CA 93908
Phone: (408) 484-0536
Fax: (408) 484-0534

Charlton Outdoor Technologies
1179-A Water Tank Road
Burlington, WA 98233
Phone: (360) 757-2608
Fax: (360) 757-2610

Cortland Line Company
3736 Kellogg Road
PO Box 5588
Cortland, NY 13045
Phone: (607) 756-2851
Web: www.cortlandline.com
/cortland

Fenwick Outdoor Technologies
Group
1900 18th Street
Spirit Lake, IO 51360
Phone: (712) 336-1520
Web: www.fenwickfishing.com

Fin-Nor/United Sports Specialists
Corp.
5553 Anglers Avenue, Suite 109-
110
Ft. Lauderdale, FL 33312
Phone: (800) 466-5507
Fax: (954) 966-5509

Hardy USA
PO Box 3987
Evergreen, CO 80437
Phone: (888) HARDYUSA
Fax: (303) 679-9090
Web: www.hardyusa.com

Islander Reels
Phone: (250) 544-1440
Fax: (250) 544-1450
Web: www.islander.com

Lamson
PO Box 469
Redmond, WA 98073
Phone: (425) 881-0733
*Lamson reels are gaining in popu-
larity, and rightfully so: They are
excellent reels, tough and dependable under stress. (Lamson is a
division of Sage; if you want to buy
a reel, contact Sage directly; for
repairs, contact Lamson.)*

L.L. Bean, Inc.
Casco Street
Freeport, ME 04033
Phone: (800) 221-4221
Fax: (207) 552-3080
Web: www.llbean.com/fish
*L.L. Bean reels run from inexpensive
to new reels like the excellent Aquis.
You can't miss.*

Marryat USA
2601 Elliot Avenue, Suite 3215
Seattle, WA 98121
Phone: (800) 578-6226
Fax: (206) 441-5590
Web: www.marryat.com

The Orvis Company, Inc.
Historic Route 7A
Manchester, VT 05254
Phone: (800) 548-9548
Fax: (540) 343-7053
Web: www.orvis.com
*Charles Orvis was the father of
modern fly reels. Truly superior
reels.*

Peerless Reel Company
427-3 Amherst Street, Suite 177
Nashua, NH 03063
Phone: (603) 595-2458
Fax: (603) 595-2458

Penn Fishing Tackle Mfg. Co.
3028 West Hunting Park Avenue
Philadelphia, PA 19132
Phone: (215) 229-9415
*Penn, although more often associ-
ated with trolling and spinning
reels, makes excellent fly reels.*

Phos Precision Fly Reels
601 Maple Avenue
Carpinteria, CA 93013
Phone: (888) 829-9399
Fax: (805) 684-6863

Precision Reels
113 Walters Avenue
Ewing, NJ 08638
Phone: (800) 555-2603
Fax: (609) 538-0510

Redington Fly Rods and Reels
906 South Dixie Highway
Stuart, FL 34994
Phone: (800) 253-2538
Fax: (561) 220-9957
Web: www.redington.com

Robichaud Reels
PO Box 119
Hudson, NH 03051
Phone: (603) 880-6484
Web: www.flyreels.com

Ross Reels
One Ponderosa Court
Montrose, CO 81401
Phone: (800) 336-1050
Fax: (970) 249-1834
Web: www.ross-reels.com
The Ross Reel is one of my all-time favorites, even in salt water. I have used their Cimarron and Gunnison Series reels under extreme conditions and find them one of the best reels available, even though they are substantially less expensive than other reels of equal caliber.

Sage Mfg. Corp.
8500 Northeast Day Road
Bainbridge Island, WA 98110
Phone: (800) 533-3004
Fax: (206) 842-6830
Web: www.sageflyfish.com
Sage's new 5000 Series reels are top notch. Sage also owns Lamson, which it bought a few years ago.

Seamaster
16115 SW 117th Avenue,
Suite A-8
Miami, FL 33177
Phone: (305) 253-2408
Fax: (305) 253-5901
Web: www.seamaster.com

STEELFIN
4714 Del Prado Boulevard
Cape Coral, FL 33904
Phone: (941) 540-9822
Fax: (941) 540-9822

STH Reels
Cortland Line Company
3736 Kellogg Road
PO Box 5588
Cortland, NY 13045
Phone: (607) 756-2851
Web: www.cortlandline.com /cortland

Teton Fly Reels
924-A2 Church Hill Road
San Andreas, CA 95249
Phone: (800) 831-0855
Fax: (209) 754-4716
Web: www.teton.com

3M Scientific Anglers
3M Center
Bldg. 223-4N-05
St. Paul, MN 55144
Phone: (800) 430-5000
Web: www.mmm.com
Scientific Anglers is always developing new reels, and they make some very affordable but still high quality reels.

Tibor Reel Corp.
900 NE 40th Court
Oakland Park, FL 33334
Phone: (954) 566-0222
Fax: (954) 566-9847

Appendix C:
Lines, Leaders, Tippet, and Backing

Airflo/Main Stream Angling
65 New Litchfield Street
Torrington, CT 06790
Phone: (860) 489-4993
Fax: (860) 496-0267

Cortland Line Company
3736 Kellogg Road
PO Box 5588
Cortland, NY 13045
Phone: (607) 756-2851
Web: www.cortlandline.com
/cortland

Fenwick Outdoor Technologies
Group
1900 18th Street
Spirit Lake, IO 51360
Phone: (712) 336-1520
Web: www.fenwickfishing.com

Gudebrod
PO Box 357
Pottstown, PA 19464
Phone: (610) 327-4050
Fax: (610) 327-4588

L.L. Bean, Inc.
Casco Street
Freeport, ME 04033
Phone: (800) 221-4221
Fax: (207) 552-3080
Web: www.llbean.com/fish

The Orvis Company, Inc.
Historic Route 7A
Manchester, VT 05254
Phone: (800) 548-9548
Fax: (540) 343-7053
Web: www.orvis.com

RIO Products
5050 Yellowstone Highway
Idaho Falls, ID 83402
Phone: (800) 553-0838
Fax: (285) 524-7763

Royal Wulff Products
3 Main Street
PO Box 948
Livingston Manor, NY 12758
Phone: (800) 328-3638
Fax: (914) 439-8055

3M Scientific Anglers
3M Center
Bldg. 223-4N-05
St. Paul, MN 55144
Phone: (800) 430-5000

Appendix D:
Flies and Fly-Tying Materials and Tools

A.K.'s Fly Tying Tools
PO Box 6250
Annapolis, MD 21401
Phone: (410) 573-0287
Fax: (410) 573-0993

Bob Marriott's Flyfishing Store
2700 West Orangethorpe Avenue
Fullerton, CA 92833
Phone: (800) 535-6633
Fax: (714) 525-5783
Web: www.bobmarriotts.com

Dan Bailey's
PO Box 1019
Livingston, MT 59047
Phone: (800) 356-4052
Fax: (406) 222-8450
Web: www.dan-bailey.com

Feather-Craft Fly-Fishing
8307 Manchester Road
St. Louis, MO 63144
Phone: (800) 659-1707
Fax: (314) 963-0324

The Fly Shop
4140 Churn Creek Road
Redding, CA 96002
Phone: (800) 669-FISH
Fax: (916) 222-3572
Web: www.theflyshop.com

The Hook & Hackle Company
7 Kaycee Loop Road
Plattsburgh, NY 12901
Phone: (800) 552-8342
Fax: (518) 561-0336
Web: www.hookhack.com

K&K Flyfisher's Supply
8643 Grant
Overland Park, KS 66212
Phone: (800) 795-8118
Fax: (913) 341-1252
Web: kkflyfisher.com

Kaufmann's Streamborn
PO Box 23032
Portland, OR 97281
Phone: (800) 442-4FLY
Fax: (503) 684-7025
Web: www.kman.com

Kennebec River Fly & Tackle Co.
39 Milliken Road
North Yarmouth, ME 04097
Phone: (207) 829-4290
Fax: (207) 829-6002

L.L. Bean, Inc.
Casco Street
Freeport, ME 04033
Phone: (800) 221-4221
Fax: (207) 552-3080
Web: www.llbean.com/fish

On The Fly
3628 Sage Drive
Rockford, IL 61114
Phone: (800) 232-9359
Fax: (815) 877-4682

The Orvis Company, Inc.
Historic Route 7A
Manchester, VT 05254
Phone: (800) 548-9548
Fax: (540) 343-7053
Web: www.orvis.com

Regal Engineering
RFD 2
Tully Road
Orange, MA 01364
Phone: (508) 575-0488

US Fly Tiers
PO Box 4374
Harrisburg, PA 17111
Phone: (717) 657-9717

Appendix E:
Rod Tubes and Gear Bags

Compleat Angler
1320 Marshall Lane
Helena, MT 59601
Phone: (406) 442-1973
Fax: (406) 442-9900

L.L. Bean, Inc.
Casco Street
Freeport, ME 04033
Phone: (800) 221-4221
Fax: (207) 552-3080
Web: www.llbean.com/fish

The Orvis Company, Inc.
Historic Route 7A
Manchester, VT 05254
Phone: (800) 548-9548
Fax: (540) 343-7053
Web: www.orvis.com

Wood River
2899 Agoura Road
Suite 114
Westlake Village, CA 91361
Phone: (800) 897-FISH

Appendix F: Waders

Bare Sportswear
PO Box 8110-577
Blaine, WA 98230
Phone: (800) 663-0111
Fax: (604) 530-8812

L.L. Bean, Inc.
Casco Street
Freeport, ME 04033
Phone: (800) 221-4221
Fax: (207) 552-3080
Web: www.llbean.com/fish

The Orvis Company, Inc.
Historic Route 7A
Manchester, VT 05254
Phone: (800) 548-9548
Fax: (540) 343-7053
Web: www.orvis.com

O S Systems
PO Box 1088
Scappoose, OR 97056
Phone: (503) 543-3126
Fax: (503) 543-3129

Simms Fishing Products
PO Box 3645
Bozeman, MT 59772
Phone: (406) 585-3557
Fax: (406) 585-3562

Appendix G:
Vests, Accessories, Gadgets, etc.

Bob Marriott's Flyfishing Store
2700 West Orangethorpe Avenue
Fullerton, CA 92833
Phone: (800) 535-6633
Fax: (714) 525-5783
Web: www.bobmarriotts.com

Dan Bailey's
PO Box 1019
Livingston, MT 59047
Phone: (800) 356-4052
Fax: (406) 222-8450
Web: www.dan-bailey.com

Kaufmann's Streamborn
PO Box 23032
Portland, OR 97281
Phone: (800) 442-4FLY
Fax: (503) 684-7025
Web: www.kman.com

L.L. Bean, Inc.
Casco Street
Freeport, ME 04033
Phone: (800) 221-4221
Fax: (207) 552-3080
Web: www.llbean.com/fish

The Orvis Company, Inc.
Historic Route 7A
Manchester, VT 05254
Phone: (800) 548-9548
Fax: (540) 343-7053
Web: www.orvis.com

Sage Mfg. Corp.
8500 Northeast Day Road
Bainbridge Island, WA 98110
Phone: (800) 533-3004
Fax: (206) 842-6830

Appendix H:
Float Tubes

L.L. Bean, Inc.
Casco Street
Freeport, ME 04033
Phone: (800) 221-4221
Fax: (207) 552-3080
Web: www.llbean.com/fish

The Orvis Company, Inc.
Historic Route 7A
Manchester, VT 05254
Phone: (800) 548-9548
Fax: (540) 343-7053
Web: www.orvis.com

Trout Traps
9860 West 59th Place
Arvada, CO 80004
Phone: (800) 831-6398
Fax: (303) 940-0310
Web: www.trouttraps.com
Trout Traps float tubes are my personal favorite. I have been using one for quite some time and have never been disappointed. They are innovative and dependable, and you really can't go wrong.

Appendix I:
Fly - Fishing Schools

Al Caucci
RD#1 Box 102
Tannersville, PA 18372
Phone: (717) 629-2962
Fax: (717) 629-2962
Web: www.mayfly.com

L.L. Bean, Inc.
Casco Street
Freeport, ME 04033
Phone: (800) 221-4221
Fax: (207) 552-3080
Web: www.llbean.com/fish

The Orvis Company, Inc.
Historic Route 7A
Manchester, VT 05254
Phone: (800) 548-9548
Fax: (540) 343-7053
Web: www.orvis.com

Sage Mfg. Co.
8500 Northeast Day Road
Bainbridge Island, WA 98110
Phone: (800) 533-3004
Fax: (206) 842-6830
Web: www.sageflyfish.com

Appendix J:
Fly-Fishing and Conservation Organizations

American Rivers
1025 Vermont Avenue, NW,
Suite 720
Washington, D.C. 20005
Phone: (800) 296-6900
Web: www.amrivers.org/amrivers

Federation of Fly Fishers
PO Box 1595
Bozeman, MT 59771
Phone: (406) 585-7592
Web: www.fedflyfishers.org

The Nature Conservancy
1815 North Lynn Street
Arlington, VA 22209
Phone: (703) 841-5300
Web: www.tnc.org

Trout Unlimited, Canada
PO Box 6270, Station D
Calgary, Alberta T2P 2C8
Phone: (800) 909-6040
Web: www.cadvision.com/tuc

Trout Unlimited
1500 Wilson Boulevard,
Suite 310
Arlington, VA 22209
Phone: (703) 522-0200
Web: www.tu.org/index.html

Appendix K:
Web Sites

Web sites change rapidly and new ones seem to be added daily. This is a list of the most important; many offer links to other sites.

Anglers On Line: www.streamside.com
Atlantic Salmon Federation: www.flyfishing.com/asf
Federation of Fly Fishers: www.fedflyfish.org
Fly Fish America Magazine: www.flyfishamerica.com
Fly Fish.Com: flyfish.com
Fly Fishers Online: www.flyfishers.com
Fly Fishing Network: www.fbn-flyfish.com
Fly Fishing in Salt Waters: www.flyfishinsalt.com
New England Salmon Association: www.flyfishing.com/nesa
North American Fishing Club: www.cvc.com/ctg/cgi-bin/nafc
Trout Unlimited: www.tu.org/index.html

Index